From Aston to Aussie

Adventures of a £10;00 Pom

Graham V Twist

AuthorHouse™
1663 Liberty Drive
Bloomington, IN 47403
www.authorhouse.com
Phone: 1-800-839-8640

©2010 Graham V Twist. All rights reserved.

No part of this book may be reproduced, stored in a retrieval system, or transmitted by any means without the written permission of the author.

First published by AuthorHouse   10/13/2010

ISBN: 978-1-4520-8202-8 (sc)

Printed in the United States of America
Bloomington, Indiana

This book is printed on acid-free paper.

WE ARE SAILING

It was mid February 1970 and on a cold wet foggy late afternoon at Southampton Docks, myself, my wife Sheila and our three children, Graham, Juliet, and Kezia had boarded the SS Fairsky to set sail on assisted passages for a new and we hoped better life in Australia.

Fairsky

We had caught the train early that morning from a miserable wet New St Station in Birmingham, and several of our relatives had travelled down to London with us, probably to make sure we were really going. After a very tearful and emotional goodbye they left, we caught the train to Southampton and were finally on our own. After we arrived we were taken on board the ship with our luggage which consisted of three suitcases and a large box full of Xmas toys for the kids. When things on the ship had settled down we found that we had been given berths on the lowest deck on the ship, which was well below the waterline as it turned out. The steward had put Sheila and the kids into one cabin and myself into one with three other blokes. There was no way we were going to travel for the next four or five weeks split up like this so Sheila said I'll put the two little ones together and you can have their bunk. Situation resolved, I went back to the cabin I was supposed to be in and told my erstwhile companions that I would be down the corridor. Sheila was unpacking and getting the cabin ready for us so I decided I wanted to see England for what could well be my final time and went back up onto the top deck of the ship. The deck was absolutely crowded but I managed to be able to get a place by the handrail, suddenly and silently without warning the Fairsky pulled by two tugs lurched and started to move slowly away from the dock. A silence descended on the highly emotional crowd of captive would be émigrés as everyone realised there was no going back now, the condensation of breaths and tears adding to the miserable fog and dampness. No room for second thoughts now, all doubts had to be forced away from your mind, fears that you may not see any of your loved ones again tried to crowd into your mind and had to be resisted. We were off.

At the stern of the ship someone had tied a huge yard round bundle of ladies nylon stockings to the handrail of the Fairsky, and as it started to move so this bundle of stockings slowly began to unwind. Meanwhile people were still throwing paper streamers both onto and off the ship it didn't seem to matter who caught them because we were all literally in the same boat, people clutched at these fragile pieces of paper as if their very lives depended on keeping some sort of contact with our homeland. Union Jack flags and red white and blue bunting were in abundance, whistles blew and horns honked. Shouts of encouragement and last goodbyes echoed around as slowly the docks began to recede into the fog, and the lights along the quayside began to get dimmer and dimmer, we could still hear people shouting but the sound was slowly fading as we went further out. The fog was low lying and from our vantage point on the top deck the words "Southampton Docks" could be seen floating eerily above the fog line dimly lit by ghostly yellow bulbs.

Boarding the Fairsky 1970

Now the only remaining contact with England was this tenuous ball of ladies stockings, and with the mournful sound of the ships foghorn and the rapidly unwinding diminishing pile of stockings emotions were really running high. By this time all sounds from the docks muffled by the fog had ceased, the lights had vanished, and England was no longer in sight or sound, we were cocooned in a ball of cotton wool fog, and the only sound on board was the muffled sound of sniffs and sobs. By now all eyes were clamped on the shrinking bundle of stockings spinning and turning like a demented animal, finally the ball had gone and everyone's eyes were riveted on the ever tightening line of stockings still attached like a nylon umbilical cord to our England, and then suddenly the line snapped with a twang and there was a collective groan and a lot of tears as the stockings vanished and took with them my heart.

What had led to this highly emotional turn of events had been a five-shilling bet with a mate of mine some two years earlier, we had been sitting in our local social club in Handsworth Birmingham in the middle of a snowy cold wet miserable night, when in a drunken moment he had challenged me to emigrate with him to Australia. Equally drunkenly I had accepted his bet, it wasn't till a week later when he had produced information on emigrating to Aussie that I realised he was serious. Now things took on a different slant, one I had taken on the bet in front of all our mates, and two, the thought of going overseas didn't seem to bother me one bit. I was a pipe fitter welder and had travelled the length and breadth of England, Scotland and Wales working away from home at least nine months out of every year, what could be the difference in working out of town in Aussie? The thought of being a heating engineer in a very hot country hadn't entered my head.

When I got the chance after discussing it all with Sheila and she agreeing I filled in the forms and then promptly forgot about them whilst working away from home. After about nine months we finally got a reply to our application, we were to go to see a Doctor nominated by the Australian Immigration Department to have a physical examination; all the family was to attend. I had to fork out for the price of this medical and it cost us over £7;00 almost a weeks wage in those days, I was a bit miffed about the medical because all he seemed to do was to make sure we were white and not obviously dying from some sort of virulent disease. And I was really narked when he told me he had a bad back. "Physician heal thyself," I told him, he didn't seem too amused with this remark and muttering to himself sent us off.

Perhaps I had got up the Doctors nose because we didn't hear again from the Immigration Office for another six months. When we finally got the call we had to go to the Immigration Office, which was overlooking the Bull Ring on the Smallbrook Ringway. The Immigration Officer was a terse red haired young man in his early thirties; and he questioned us in depth as to why we wanted to emigrate, our motives, hopes, and aspirations. We must have hit the right buttons because after about an hour he pulled out a folder, right Mr and Mrs Twist I can have you on a plane and in Sydney in six weeks, my stomach suddenly turned to water it was the moment of truth and it had come too quick. We don't want to go to Sydney I said, this didn't seem to faze him too much; OK he said looking in the folder once more. I can have you in Melbourne in seven weeks is that all right he asked as he decisively closed the folder on our future. We don't want to go to Melbourne I told him, and this time I really got his attention and his professional smile began to slip just a bit. Can you tell me why you don't want to go to either Sydney or Melbourne? he asked through what I thought were the beginnings of clenched teeth. That's easy I said just turn around and look out of the window, this is my home town and it is a big city, and in this big city of mine I am an absolute nobody, apart from family and friends and workmates I may as well not exist, and if I am going to make good in Australia then I feel I have to go somewhere where we will have a chance, and having looked at lots of places we think that Adelaide might be the place for us. He appeared to take this on board and giving the slightest of sighs he re-opened the dreaded flying folder which seemed to be full of empty seats just waiting for the Twist family. He took a deep breath, right, there is a flight to Adelaide in six weeks, is that OK he said daring me I thought to say no. By now he had got me on the back foot and my brain was spinning whilst I tried to find a way around this mans obvious by now burning desire to get us on a plane and out of his sight. We don't want to fly we want to go by boat I told him, this time he very nearly did have a fit, by boat he asked, yes please I said. He tried I thought to emphasise his displeasure at my request by slamming down the flying folder but being cardboard it acted like a bellows and he only succeeded in blowing some other paperwork off his desk. He slowly bent down to pick them up, I cant make the ship arrangements from here today, thank you for calling we will be in touch. I noticed that his mouth said one thing but his eyes and body language said another.

That was in about April 1969, we heard nothing again for months and all thoughts of going to Aussie were slowly fading when we had a telegram in late November 1969, that simply said your ship the "The Fairsky sails from Southampton Docks on the 19th January to Adelaide, please contact this office for further travel directions. The red haired man with the flying folder had finally got one over us. At this time we were living in a £3;00 a week two up two down rented terraced house, with an outside toilet, and no heating apart from coal fires, it was that cold in the Winter that the steam from your breath at night would freeze up on the insides of the windows. This house was in Oakfield Avenue, Booth Street, Handsworth. We had been on the Birmingham City Housing Department list for eight years, and despite having three kids and living in and working all our lives in Birmingham we had never had an offer of a place off the council. We like thousands of other Brummies had lived in rooms, we went from a single rented room in Booth Street Handsworth, then to Erdington with my mom, then to Sheila's moms in Handsworth, then to my sisters in Miller Street Aston, then to one room in Sandwell Road Handsworth, then to three rooms on the Birchfield Road, and then to the house we were now in. I had had many a battle with the Birmingham City Housing Department and all to no avail; even when our second child was born prematurely in cold damp conditions, our requests fell on heartless deaf ears. It seemed to me that even then new immigrants were getting preference over the local population. This may have had a bearing on our decision to go to Australia to seek a better life. Handsworth was a nice place to live in at the time but it was obvious things were changing rapidly. To vacate the house all I had to do was give a couple of weeks notice to the man we rented the place off and we would be gone. Obviously we had a house full of furniture, clothes, bed linen, domestic appliances and all the paraphernalia that goes with having a house with three young kids. During my travels by trains and buses over the years and being a prolific reader I had gathered hundreds of books, and as I was the only one that had read them they were mostly in good condition. I went to a second-hand book shop on the Soho Road with ten books that were worth about a fiver new and all they offered me was half a crown for the lot, needless to say I didn't accept the measly price and gave them all away to my mates and drinking companions at the local pubs.

Typical back to back houses, I lived in the house in the background with sister in law Joan and husband Leo.

We had finally got rid of all but the bare essentials a week before we were due to go, all we had to take with us was a big box of Christmas toys for the kids and three cases of clothes we thought we might need, including overcoats, fur boots, macs woollen jumpers and all the things necessary for living in a hot dry climate. Then we had another telegram. The ship has been held up and it wont be sailing till the third of February it said. I felt like the man with the flying folder was laughing his eyeteeth out at us.

My mate in the meantime had been keeping me up to date with his application and seemed to have no fears or doubts about going overseas. They had been due to go in late December, and when no one saw him after that date we all assumed they had gone. He'd gone all right, gone into hiding that is. I never found out till I got a letter off one of my drinking partners from up the club that he had bottled out. He was ostracised by my other mates for a while then they all went back to how things had been, boozing, fishing, football and all minus me. It took me a long time to get my five bob off him but eventually I did it in the end.

Our last night in England.

ON BOARD SHIP.

So, on board ship things had taken a sudden drastic change for the worse, we hadn't been at sea for an hour and had just reached open seas when Sheila was violently seasick. I finally got the ships Doctor to have a look at her, Hmm he said as he gave her an injection in her bum, you have bruised your bottom, Sheila hadn't got the heart to tell him it was a love bite I had inflicted on her a few nights before. The first night on this ship at sea was revelation to say the least, being on the lowest deck when you lay in your bunk you were thrown and rolled all over the place, we had to put the rails up the sides of the bunks so that we wouldn't get thrown out of them. One minute you were lying level then your feet would be above your head, then you would be swung violently from side to side, and all the time this was accompanied by tremendous noises that sounded like Father Neptune was using a sledgehammer to try to get to you. It was like being drunk without having a beer, and the words "spinning like a top" took on a whole new meaning that night.

The next morning out of our family only myself and Kezia the youngest were in a fit state to venture up top for some breakfast, the gut wrenching eye watering smell of spew and vomit, and other uncontrolled bodily functions as we travelled up from the bowels of the ship was horrendous, I am convinced to this day that the crew deliberately didn't clean up the spew that swirled around the corridors until everyone had retched themselves dry. Still this plan seemed to work because when we got to the Bay of Biscay some days later on the waves were massive and although the ship swung and slewed about like a cork on water, nobody seemed really bothered. The breakfast room only had six or seven other brave people in it when we got there, and having been shown to our table, which was going be ours for the rest of the trip I wondered why there was a two inch piece of wood sticking up all around the top edge of the table, I asked for a menu. Would you like the eggs and bacon sir asked the leering steward looking I thought for any signs of weakness in me, yes please and some sausages and fried bread and tomatoes, this bloke had obviously never met a rough tough travelling construction worker from the back streets of Aston and Handsworth. I had lived in some real rough digs, and to have a clean white tablecloth as you ate your breakfast was a pleasure. Kezia had cornflakes and suddenly the secret of the wooden up stand was revealed when the ship took an almighty lurch and her bowl flew to the far side of the table, the up stand was there to stop the crockery and things flying off the table in rough weather, what it didn't stop was the cornflakes and milk landing on the floor. From where we sat everything appeared level, so it was a strange sight to see her breakfast dish slide to the edge of the table then slowly as if tipped by an invisible hand empty itself over the side.

For me life on board this ship was like one long holiday, to make ends meet and to try to bring up our three kids in a half decent manner, Sheila had to work, and all my life when I had the chance I had had to graft seven days a week, twelve to fourteen hours a day being the norm mostly out of town and in digs that sometimes you wouldn't put a dog into. Living on chips and boozing every night was normal, you would do your twelve or so hours then a quick bag of chips on the way back to the digs, a wash a change and then out on the booze. This trip certainly showed you how the other half lived, and I was jealous. We had never been able to afford to go on holiday ourselves and the only time we had got away was to Great Yarmouth on a huge caravan site. And this was only when Sheila's dad had passed away and her mom had paid for us to go for two weeks. Needless to say our spending money was gone after the first week and I had to tap up the brother in law for a few quid. It was the weeks of the world cup and the camp had a couple of small TV rooms, there being none in the caravans, I bought a book and three hours before the final went to one of these rooms at twelve o'clock and got the last seat in there, the kick off was at three. Buried in the book I hardly noticed any one else in the room so it was a real surprise to me when I finally looked up. The room was jam packed and there were blokes outside standing on beer barrels looking and shouting through the windows and door. So I watched England win the World Cup live on the telly surrounded by peed up cockneys and all of us yelling Engerland, Engerland fantastic. I like everyone in that room was so proud to be English that day.

It was on this ship that I learned where the word posh came from, on the ships notice board one day there was a note saying you could hire a deck chair or chairs for the rest of the trip, once you had hired these chairs and you had positioned them they were to remain yours and in that place for the whole journey. While I was in the queue waiting to hire a couple of chairs I had got talking to a big six foot two or three bloke. We had quite a rattle and he said when you get your chairs follow me, this I did and instead of going where lots of the others were going we went to the opposite side of the ship. They will be frying when we get to the Equator he told me, here's where we need to be. **Port Outward Starboard Home**. This giant of a man had been a sub-mariner for the last eighteen years and was taking his family to a new life in Queensland. Like most big blokes he was a real nice man when we got to know him, he was looking forward to starting a new life like all of us, and after eighteen years in submarines it seemed he couldn't get enough his family and of the fresh sea air. Everyday at ten o'clock he would go to the bar for his tot of rum, he liked a drink but I never saw him drunk. There was plenty to do on board, you could play deck quoits, cards, table tennis, chess, have a go at shooting clay pigeons, and run round the decks if you were up to it. There was a small pool for the little kids and a bigger on for the grown ups. They had a map of the world pinned on a wall and every day they would plot where the ship was, you could also have a bet as to how many miles you thought the ship might travel the next day, it was usually around four hundred and fifty or so subject to weather conditions. Our first port of call was Las Palmas, our first time on real foreign soil, We went on shore and I tried to walk around as if I had done this sort of thing all my life, but I think our white faces and woollen jumpers had somehow given us away as new suckers for the local wide boys to fleece. The weather was great, the sun shining and with a warm breeze ruffling your hair life couldn't be better. Landing here gave us a chance to replace the new shoes that Graham had had to travel in. He had taken a mighty kick at a ball one day and his shoe had flown over the top of the handrail and into the sea. We were followed around by a Spanish bloke trying to flog me a watch, you a big man he said, you have got three kids, he had obviously mistaken us for people of culture and wealth who had the money to go on mid winter ships cruises, a few well chosen choice words between us soon dispelled this idea, and at my invitation to walk away in a funny fashion, he ambled away from my uncouth Brummagem Summer Lane language trying to find some better tempered easier clients.

Over the next few days the weather got better and temperature really went up and one day in my ignorance, my only excuse I suppose was that the sun didn't shine like this in Brum. I had gone onto the top deck, laid down on a towel and had promptly gone to sleep, waking up a couple of hours later I found that my front had turned a bright tomato red, whilst my back remained a pasty white. The sun had given me what seemed like second-degree burns, it was that fierce it had had burnt the skin off my eyelids and it was very painful to walk. I was too embarrassed to go to the Doctors with my barber's pole new look and spent a couple of days or so hidden below decks. When I finally plucked up the courage to go back up on deck the skin that had been abused, in protest at my stupidity hung off me in strips, little Kezia spent hours pulling off long pieces of this dead skin. After that first taste of what the Sun can do I never seemed to have any trouble at all with sunburns, and later on worked in desert heats of between forty five and fifty degrees centigrade with no side effects at all. It was a very painful lesson at the time but it served me well in the future.

Outside the back of our two up two down rented house 1969.

The food we ate on board was the same as the paying passengers, and having been brought up on good honest fare some of it appeared to be really fancy to us. Every Saturday night there was a special meal and then a dance, as ten pound tourists we didn't get invited to the Captains table but then I suppose that would have been just a little too much to ask. We crossed the equator and the crew did the time honoured play about Neptune. Not something seen by everyone and we all got a certificate to prove we had made the crossing. We spent our time lazing about sitting on our deckchairs, trying to keep cool, watching the flying fish skim above the waves, porpoise surfed on the bow waves and there was the occasional sight of a whale, or another ship. There was a laundry on board where items of clothing could be washed, and with three kids to look after Sheila used it quite regularly, that is until one day some thieving swine stole all her washing including the girls dresses and my Tee shirts off the line. Talk about desperate people. I left a note in the laundry offering other things to the thieves if they wanted to come to our cabin but not surprisingly no one took up the offer. Cape Town was the next port of call, when we got there we were kept out at sea for quite a while until the ship docked and then we were then allowed off in groups, because of the shortness of time left we decided to go on a coach trip around Table Top Mountain, the view from the top over Cape Town was magnificent, and in the darkening warm South African night the city lights twinkled and sparkled like glow worms, we could see our ship like a tiny model toy in the docks, and the velvet darkness of the night hid the shanty towns, and the rough rusting corrugated tin huts of the indigenous Africans. When we returned to the Fairsky and it set sail the abiding memory of Cape Town as it slowly vanished over the stern of the ship was that Table Top Mountain was lit up with massive searchlights, a fantastic sight and a truly beautiful thing to see.

Looking forward to a new future on Board Fairsky 1970.

A few nights out of Cape Town after going round the stormy Cape of Good Hope and by now none of the sea and ship hardened travellers batted an eyelid, even when a huge wave hit the side of the ship one day tipping it over at such an angle that one minute I was looking at the blue sky and then suddenly down into the bottomless green sea, this wave sent all the furniture in the lounge flying to one side trapping and breaking some poor blokes leg. A chap from Wolverhampton, his wife and four children had been allocated to our dinner table, and we got to know them really well, they were also going to Adelaide and we would spend hours musing on what it was going to be like. I must admit I hadn't read a thing about the place I just wanted the whole experience to smack me full in the face. One day the two of us whilst taking our usual stroll around the decks had noticed the crew putting up sheeting all around the ships handrails and sides. We asked them what this was for and one of them said there was a big storm blowing up. That night down in the bowels of the ship it began to get worse than it had ever been before, the slewing and spinning effect was bad and the sledgehammer blows of the waves kept us awake, Sheila and the kids were hidden under the blankets and were not going anywhere. I went and got my new Wolverhampton mate and we made our way to the top deck of the ship which hadn't got any sheeted protection and was open to the elements. We went as far forward as we could get and because the ship was rolling from side to side we hung onto the handrails for sheer life. What a magnificent sight greeted us, rain, thunder and lightening, huge seas and spray that went right over our heads even though we were some seventy feet above sea level. The white capped massive waves seemed to be coming at the ship from different angles and we could see that the helmsman was turning the ship into the waves to meet them head on, the ship would seem to surf down the side of the wave and then plough up into the oncoming seemingly vertical wall of water. Whoever was at the wheel certainly knew his job and handled the ship superbly so that we felt no real fear at all. It was a wet and cold windy night but it was one I will never forget, when dawn came we were stiff with cold and salt spray had spiked up our hair like mad, but we were enthralled. Nature when it is like this is awesome, and we were lucky to see it in all its magnificent glory.

Kezia shows her all

On a Saturday evening a couple of nights after the storm they put on a hippy night, everyone got dressed up in the early sixties style and the night was a great success, I had a big paper flower sewn onto the front of my jeans and paying a visit to the toilet I had met the sub-mariner, what you got behind that flower man, he asked with a laugh, I cant tell you sailor boy was the reply.

Our new Captain Graham, driving the Fairsky.

Early the next morning the ships alarms went off and the crew came round and did a head count of all the male passengers, I was obviously in the wrong cabin but they must have known this and when they were told my name they ticked it off a list without comment and then hurried off. Going to breakfast later on in the morning all sorts of rumours were rife from someone being stabbed to someone else being thrown over board, the reality when it came out was much worse, two passengers and one crew member had been by the front of the ship when a man who had been leaning against the handrail suddenly fell overboard. He would have had to be a big man because the handrail was at least four feet high. The alarm was raised immediately and the Officer of the watch told what had happened, they slowed down the ship but did not lower a boat or make any other obvious apparent attempt to rescue the person. The person who had gone over the side was my mate the sub-mariner, we were absolutely devastated and when I angrily asked one of the crew why they hadn't stopped and lowered a boat he got a box of rubbish and threw it into the sea at the spot where the sub-mariner had gone over the side. The box flew down the side of the ship and then was pulled under the back of the ship and into the propellers leaving nothing but a few bits and pieces in the wake of the ship. It seemed that they all thought that there would have been no chance of survival for the sub-mariner, but I still wake up occasionally at night even now thinking that this man had been highly trained to react to any sort of danger especially around water. What if as soon as he hit the water he had managed to swim away from the danger of the propellers which he must have known about, what if he had got away and then watched the ship sailing off towards the horizon, what would his thoughts have been if he just floated there thinking of his family who he so obviously loved deeply but had hardly seen and their life without him in a new land. Who would look after them, what would they do. It was a terrible, horrible, lonely way to go, especially to be left by your own sea faring kind, and I only hope and pray that he did go under the props and died instantly.

They held a memorial at sea for the sub-mariner, something that is very rarely seen by most people, and this time they stopped the ship and we threw wreaths into the sea. We shed a tear or two for our newly found newly lost mate. The crew all gave up a days pay in respect of a fellow sailor and there were collections and raffles on his family's behalf. The ships owners also offered to take his family back to England for free, an offer that was accepted by his widow.

Hippy night.

Apparently because of the upset it caused the Captain must have thought it would be a good idea to divert the ship and sail past some land to give his passengers something else to think about, the land he chose was a tiny speck on the map, it was called Isle St Paul a thousand miles from anywhere. This little bit of land in the middle of the vast Indian Ocean was shaped like the top of a volcano that had turned on its side, it created a perfect safe harbour lagoon in the middle of the vast ocean, and anchored in that lagoon was a fishing trawler. The trawler men seemed to be jumping up and down and waving to us so everybody was waving back at the obviously friendly fishermen, it wasn't till I turned my binoculars around to the horizon and saw their buoys stretched right across the sea in front of us that I knew why they were waving. The ship sailed right through the fishing lines cutting them and setting the buoys adrift with no hesitation at all. Another fine example of sea going courtesy!

THE CAMP.

The eastern coast of Australia and Freemantle slowly appeared through the heat haze in the distance, our first port of call in our new promised land. The Sunday we landed was beautiful, clear blue sky and a nice warm breeze. As we came down the ramp off the ship Customs and Excise were there to greet us, G,day sir where's your Moe? I was dumbfounded, Moe, how did he know the brother in laws girl friend Moe? It was a mystery to me so I said I think she is still in the UK with John . He sighed and pointed to our Document of Identity, which had Sheila's photo on it as well as mine, your mo he said indicating my Viva Zapata moustache, oh I shaved that off ages ago. His attempt at being nice to this newcomer to his shores falling on ignorant ears he checked we hadn't got any illegal fruit or other dangerous guns or foodstuffs then waved us on. The first thing we bought for the kids and ourselves were ice creams, they were delicious, it was so warm we had to take our coats off, it would take a real long time to get used to the weather and not going out prepared for rain, snow or shine. Perth looked to be a wonderful place its pristine tall buildings bathed in the bright sunlight, people going to church and everywhere so different and clean and tidy compared to Aston and Handsworth where we had come from. Various Australian Banks and Financial Companies joined the ship at this point and you were invited to start an account or whatever with them. But only having a few quid I declined their offers, I didn't want anyone to know we were skint. After nearly five weeks of living like Lords the bubble finally had to burst, and it did so in a spectacular fashion. Three days later and we landed at Port Adelaide South Australia where we spent the night anchored out at sea waiting to get into port. When all our papers had been checked we were put on what the Aussies called a coach, this consisted of a front engine that reversed under a trailer that was built like a coach. From where I sat I had a clear view of the driver and when he took off I noticed that he drove off the main road and went around what I found out later was the real rough part of the port and its surroundings. Most of the buildings were built out of red rusty corrugated sheets of iron, There were derelict houses and factories and the whole area was a dilapidated mess. I heard a broad Black Country voice say I don't loik it ere, followed by one or two voices agreeing, I looked into the drivers eyes through the mirror he was listening to us on the radio and he was laughing so I knew this was a wind up. Finally we arrived at the camp where we would spend the next fourteen or so weeks, we were welcomed by the man we immediately called "The Commandant" he didn't mince his words, just a few pointers he said. One, don't drink the water straight from the taps, the water in Adelaide was that bad back then even the ships refused to take on water from there, sometimes when it came out of the taps it was brown. Two, if you take any food outside look out for blowflies, these large flies could produce live maggots onto any food and in no time your food would be awash with tiny wriggling white maggots. Three. Look out for snakes; the camp was on the edge of Adelaide Airport so there was plenty of nasty bits of wildlife about. Four. Watch out for the Red Back Spider, this little charmer, which was apparently all over the place, it was coal black and had a red cross on its back, its favourite hiding place it was said was under the toilet seat, so when you went to the toilet a lot of banging of seats up and down was the norm. It was supposedly capable of killing small kids, although we never heard of any being killed by this little darling. People going out of the room after that little pep talk were walking as if on glass, periscope like eyeballs were swivelling all over the place and all the little kids were up in mom or dads arms. Subject to how many children you had decided the size of the rooms you were allowed to have. The rooms were in old Army Nissan huts presumably left on the fringes of the airport after the end of the war. The dividing walls were wooden and were that thin that if anyone broke wind the sound travelled along the huts like a wave on the beach, and could be heard by all and sundry, if there was an argument everyone could sit back and hear it. And noisy sex was an absolute no no. We took stock of our situation, we had a large box full of Xmas toys, we had three suitcases full of jumpers and lots of warm clothes, the temperature at the time being in the high eighties. We had three roughly furnished rooms in an old Army Nissan hut. We had no vehicle, I had no job, we knew no one in Australia, and we had the princely sum of five pounds in cash. OK then time to roll up the sleeves and have a go.

We had landed at the camp on a Thursday, and on Friday morning there was a bloke from the local employment office there to try to help you get a job. Lots of the people who had arrived had come over to work in a car factory about twenty miles away from the camp. They were picked up and dropped off every day and had people to help them with any problems, including buying or renting or getting a house off the local government. I sat in front of the officer, what is your job he asked, I am a heating engineer/pipe fitter welder I said proudly hoping to impress this colonial antipodean man in a far off land with my skills, what's one of those he asked. It was at this moment that I thought there might be a few problems finding a job in my trade. He finally decided that I was what was called a mechanical services plumber, that was someone who worked with steel pipes (me a plumber, the shame of it) and gave me an address of a company in Adelaide to contact. I rang this company and agreed to meet them on the Saturday, there was a slight problem with this as I had no idea as to how to get there, I didn't know how to get there by bus, I couldn't afford a taxi, I didn't know anyone who could offer me a lift, so I decided to walk it. After all it was only about an inch on the map we were given. I got up early on the Saturday and set off, being a rough tough construction worker I was well prepared for any weather problems, wearing a thick jumper and with a coat slung over one arm, and I viewed the bright blue sky with some suspicion; it was bound to rain soon. It took me two hours to walk that inch on the map, and a large outside thermometer on a building proclaimed it to be eighty five degrees, I finally got to the office and spoke to the bloke in charge, how did you get here he asked looking at my sweaty red face and my thick coat and jumper hanging casually over my arm, I walked here, he slowly shook his head in what seemed like amazement, and shouted to his mate, this bloody silly galah walked here from Glenelg, his mate snorted in derision, bloody poms, will they never learn. I felt like I was the invisible man and wanted to have a go at them for talking about me as if I didn't exist and couldn't hear what they said, and it was at that moment that I instantly understood what it was like to be a foreigner in a strange land, and I was the same colour as them, and spoke the same language. It hit home to me how hard it must be for people of a different colour who couldn't speak the local language must have felt in when they got to white countries. But I held my tongue for two reasons, one I was desperate for work, and two, he was a big six foot tall hard faced rangy aussie, After talking to him for about half an hour it became obvious that my finely honed special skills would be of no use to his company, he was looking for a domestic plumber, to work on house plumbing. I think he must have taken pity on this hot and bothered person in front of him because even though I was a silly galah, he said I will drop you back off at the camp. This offer went a long way to restoring my faith in my new countrymen. He wrote down a name and phone number, try this bloke he may be able to help you, he works with steel pipes. He clocked the mileage back to the camp; bloody hell eight miles in this weather he managed to refrain from calling me a mad pommy bastard but then again his eyes couldn't hide his thoughts.

On the Monday I rang the number he had given me and spoke to the boss, we arranged to meet outside the camp that night. Although I spoke what I thought was perfect Queens English I had a bit of a problem getting my message through to him because of my thick Brummy accent but we managed. That Monday night right on time a pick up truck rolled up outside the camp, the driver got out, a large hand shot out to shake my hand, G, day are you Graham, I didn't realise it at the time but I had just met one of the nicest, kindest caring people that I have ever met. This man was to have a big influence on my family's future, and me and for that I am eternally grateful to him. We sat in the pickup and discussed what I could do and if it was going to be useful to him and the company he owned. He said I have never employed a Pom before so I hope this isn't going to be a mistake, I replied that I had never been employed by an Aussie before and hoped the same, he laughed at that. We both decided we could be of some mutual benefit and it then came down to money, I can only pay you $64;00 dollars a week he said, bloody hell I thought $64;00 dollars a week was roughly £32;00 a week, when I had left England as a top foreman running large projects I had only earned ten shillings an hour and if I only did forty hours that was £20;00 a week, I tried not to kiss him and rip his hand off in agreement, but suddenly thought, how many hours a week do I have to do for that sort of money I asked suspiciously. Forty was the reply. He told me to be at the main Post Office in Adelaide city centre the next morning which was where the job was at seven thirty and even gave me five dollars for my bus fare. You can catch the bus at the end of this road; it takes you right to the Post Office. I did cartwheels back to our rooms and told Sheila about how much I was going to earn and that we were on our way. I slept a bit better that night knowing I had work to start in the morning. The next morning at six thirty sharp I stood by the bus stop on the main road, a plastic box with sandwiches in it in one hand and a coat in my other hand, a Bus came along with Adelaide City centre on it, I raised my hand and the bus flew straight past me, the driver didn't even glance my way, this happened two more times and I was beginning once again to feel like the invisible man, a builders van went past, the passenger had his window down, G,day goose he shouted, I waved back at him what friendly people some of these Aussies are I thought. It was now gone seven thirty and there was no way it seemed that any of these buses was going to stop for me. Dejectedly I went back to the camp, ring him up said Sheila he might understand, this I did and he told me to wait there and he would get me picked up. The big Aussie driver when he came didn't mince his words, are you the Pommy bastard who's supposed to be at the Post Office? yes please, get in he said and took off at breakneck speed, we drove back onto the main road, why don't the buses stop for you over here I asked, I was stood at that bus stop for ages I said indicating the post with its round top just like the ones in Brum. The driver broke into gales of laughter and nearly drove off the road, you stupid bloody drongo that's a city limit sign. So I wasn't invisible after all, just stupid. At least it broke the ice and when he had got me into Adelaide and had told the other blokes about what had happened they all laughed that much they seemed to forget for the moment that I was a lazy, no good ten pound tourist whingeing Pom. Thus started my working life in the beautiful city of Adelaide. At about nine thirty someone started shouting Smoko and because we were welding around oil tanks I thought the place was on fire and ran outside grabbing a fire extinguisher on the way, what you doing out here one of the blokes asked, wasn't that a fire warning that Smoko thing. No mate another peal of laughter, that means we stop for a break, blimey would I ever learn this strange language. At a quarter to four the guys wrapped up the tools, I've been told to make sure you get back to the camp OK, so jump in the pickup. When I got back I was that early to be home Sheila asked me if I had packed up the job, back in the UK it would be seven or eight o'clock usually. It was amazing there we were within about half a mile of a beach, three hours of daylight left, weather warm but a little hazy, I took Graham down to the beach and we stripped off our tops, two hours later we were back in the camp, having walked a couple of miles up and down the beach.[Just a word here about working conditions on building sites in Australia which couldn't have been more different than in the UK. In the early sixties on sites in the UK if there wasn't a public toilet nearby then bad luck, mostly if there were toilets at all they were just wooden thunder boxes that would be emptied once a week if we were lucky regardless of whether they were full or not, and if you had a hundred building workers on site then ripe was not the word. I have seen the frozen shit a foot above the pan and no one ever complained. Building site workers were treated worse than animals in some cases, there were no washing facilities and if you only wanted a piss then any room on the site would do. By comparison every site in Australia however big or small had a mobile shower and flushing toilet, separate eating areas and changing rooms, this as I found out was down to the Unions and the Aussie attitude of not standing for any sort of nonsense, especially off the Bosses. No one could get onto a building site without the appropriate union card, this ensured that every man was treated the same, I had certainly had my run ins with the unions in the UK but here it was different. For instance if you didn't want to join a union because of your religion or any other reason you were allowed to donate the money it would have cost you to a charity of your choice, you had to get receipts off the charity to prove you had paid and to produce these on request but as long as you did so there was no problem with anyone. Every six weeks or so there would be union officials at the entrance to the sites and you had to show a current paid up card, failure to do so meant you didn't get on the site that day regardless of your excuses. And you would have to produce your card before you would be let back on site. It may have been oppressive in a sense but the working conditions could not be faulted.]

During that night Graham was violently sick, and came into our room, my back hurts, we turned on the light and were horrified to find his back was one complete blister. A doctor was called and although he didn't abuse me he told me in no uncertain terms what the Sun could do even if it is behind clouds, lesson learnt, and to this day Graham doesn't like the Sun too much. On the camp we had made friends with our adjoining neighbours a couple from Liverpool who had two kids, he had got a job at the car factory about twenty miles away and was just waiting for the South Australia Housing Trust to find them a house. In the meantime hardly anyone of us having transport and generally confined to camp at nights and weekends someone started up a football team. This team of ex-patriot Poms, which included the Irish, Jocks and Taffy's would take on anyone. The Italians, Greeks and Germans were certainly not backward in coming forward and there were some huge epic hours long battles, black eyes, bruises and kicked in shins being the order of the day. I can't remember who won the games but it was us who won most of the fights.

The food on this camp was not the best in the world, but then again it wasn't supposed to be, you were encouraged to get off the camp as soon as you could and this was just another way of helping you make your mind up. The exception for some reason being Sundays when it was more than palatable. So much so the Wolverhampton couple and their kids came down on some Sundays and paid for their food. You could tell the nationalities of the people who used the dining room by how and where they sat, the Brits would be on single tables, the Germans would generally put a couple of tables together and the Mediterranean's like the Italians and Greeks would all get together in one big mass. One incident sticks out in my mind about this canteen, there was a small Scotsman at the front of the queue one day and he must have felt he was being hassled by the Italians behind him. Getting obviously annoyed he turned round, back off he said or Ill give you a Glasgow kiss, unfortunately his thick Glaswegian accent meant nothing to the milling crowd of excited chattering Italians, who just glanced at him and carried on rattling, all we heard then was I told you then the sound of fist on jaw and the clatter of teeth on the floor and a toothless Italian staggered backwards, a snarl from another Italian bent on retaining Italian honour, a swishing roundhouse punch that missed and then another smack the same result and more teeth on the floor, a third larger man moved in squaring up to the little Jock like a real boxer, spitting out what sounded like obscene invective, this was like water off a ducks back to the Celtic Kid, smack and even more gleaming white teeth hit the deck. The awesome little Jock turned back to the counter, got his food and ambled away leaving the three Italians toothless and bloodied and in shock and no doubt wishing they were elsewhere. I told the football captain to get him in our side as soon as he could, and when he did play there was an invisible ring around him on the pitch which none of the opposition would enter into. Because we had nothing in the bank it was a real battle for us to get the money together to put a deposit down on one of the many houses available to rent, the wooden shack had to be paid for and suitable clothes for us all had to be bought. Sheila was great at saving but even so it still took us about fourteen weeks to get enough cash together to look for a place. In the meantime the scousers had moved twenty miles away to be by the car plant, they had been found a place by the South Australian Housing Trust. Having no transport we couldn't visit them until the man I worked for told me to take the Australian driving test, this only consisted of going to an office right by where I was working in the town and taking a written test. I passed the test and a couple of days later he rolled up in a Ute which was an open backed pick-up, it only had a bench seat at the front but we managed to squeeze everybody into it, to us it was a Godsend. he said you can have this till you can afford a car, I have filled it up for you and you can fill it up anytime you want to at my garage. Take the wife and kids sightseeing, what a gesture and what a man, and he would even suggest places for us to visit.

On the camp, sitting on the bonnet of the Ute my boss lent us.

It was about this time that I visited my first Aussie pub, it was about half a mile from the camp in a place called Glenelg, I walked there one Saturday night on my own and went into the bar, strangely although it was Saturday night there was only one other person in there, I looked at his drink, it didn't look to be a full pint to me, and when the barman asked me what I wanted I said on of those pointing to the other bloke's glass. The barman eyed me up and down, are you a Pom he asked, yes through gritted teeth, that's called a schooner he told me, and reaching under the bar pulled out a fresh ice-cold glass from the fridge and promptly filled it with what was commonly called by one and all the Amber Nectar. I had a good look around this bar and noticed a small shelf running the full length of the bar, I wondered what it was there for as there was nothing placed on it that I could see. I found out sometime later that as was the custom in Aussie that if you went for a beer two or three handed then you would put your ten or twenty dollar note on the bar, the barman would then take for your round when it was your turn, you wouldn't even have to tell him whos turn it was because he would invariably know. The shelf was there for anyone who had left their change on the bar, it would be put up on the shelf and when you next went into the pub the barman would return it to you!. I don't think you could do anything like this in the UK, and it says a lot for the honesty of the Australians. On the walls were posters claiming Kerley is King, and Carn the Bays, there were large posters of black and yellow tigers and I wondered what it was all about. It turned out that Kerley was the manager of the local Aussie rules football club, and The Bays was their war cry. I had about six or seven of these schooners which didn't seem to have much effect on me, I was not impressed too much, give me a pint of M&Bs mild any day I thought. I strolled out of the pub and promptly fell over the chain fence that ran around the car park, I rapidly revised my opinion as to the strength of the Amber Nectar.

OUR FIRST REAL PLACE.

We had been visiting the scousers over at a place called Christies Downs, this place was out in the sticks back then and consisted of a few factories, schools and housing estates, it was also right by a magnificent beach. Our other friends from Wolverhampton had gone the other way to a place, which the Aussies desparingly called Pommy Hills, its real name was Para Hills, and it was close by the biggest collection of English people in South Australia, who lived in a place called Elizabeth. named after Queen Elizabeth. I had decided long ago that when we got to Aussie we would live right amongst the true dinky di natives. I wanted a real taste of Aussie life and I knew I wouldn't get it living with my own kind. Eventually Sheila had saved enough money for us to go house hunting, house being the Aussie term because all the houses were bungalows. We decided on a place called Morphet Vale, twenty miles south of Adelaide along the South Road, which rose over the top of the Adelaide hills. You were able to stop at a place called Lookout Point and the view over the city was absolutely magnificent, Adelaide is built on a flat plain and on a clear day you could see for at least thirty miles, the city being surrounded by these hills, at nighttime it could take your breath away it was so beautiful. The house, which was a bungalow as usual, had three bedrooms, a bathroom and all the usual things including a tin corrugated roof. When it rained which was usually at night time the sound of the rain on this roof could lull you to sleep in no time, it was like being in a tent in the wet., to us coming from a tiny freezing cold damp terraced house from the back street slums of Aston and Handsworth to this detached large bungalow was like a dream come true. It even had a real garden with flowers and plants in it, something we had never had. We felt we had moved into a palace. And it was nice to have some real home cooking again. One day we went so stock up the larder and drove into a place called Reynella and while walking around looked into the local butchers window, and there hanging up was half a sheep for the ridiculous price of nine dollars, about four pounds in English money. We went in and ordered this half a sheep and the butcher cut it up into chops, legs and the like, talk about living like lords, this was big time stuff to us.

When we had left England Sheila had eventually gone off the dreaded pill. This must have upset how her body worked because whilst on the camp she stopped having periods. She finally went to see the local Doctor before we left the camp and he told her she was pregnant. Obviously on hearing that all forms of birth control had gone out of the window and we looked forward to having a real Australian child. We thought nothing more about her pregnancy, what with moving into a real place, getting the kids into the local school and all the problems associated with moving to a new area. It was about two months after we had moved that I said you don't seem to be putting on much weight for a woman who is pregnant. Sheila promptly went to the Doctors and he said to her with a great deal of pleasure congratulations Mrs Twist you are six weeks pregnant. The mistake as we called the unknown child turned out to be a little boy. When he was born he had thick corn blonde almost white hair, which we thought was unusual as we both had black hair as did his brother and sisters. It must be something in the Australian air because at the age of seven his hair went jet black as it remains so today. This strange event is common amongst Aboriginal children but it amazed us that it happened to one of our own. We had got Graham and Juliet into the local school by this time, which was only about three hundred yards away from where we lived. One day feeling fairly ill Sheila had asked Graham to wait for Juliet and to bring her home with him, normally she would have gone herself but this day she really felt poorly. At about three thirty the door went and in came Graham, where is Juliet Sheila asked, I don't know he said I didn't see her. She told him to wait in the house and to look after Kezia while she went out to find Juliet. As she walked towards the school a lady came towards her slowly down the road in a car, Sheila saw that Juliet was in the car which stopped by her, are you her mother the lady asked, yes, I'm afraid there has been an accident and she has been hurt, Sheila's legs almost gave way but she got Juliet out of the car and despite being pregnant ran carrying her back to the house. It later turned out that as she had come out of school some bigger lad had set about her, he punched her and kicked her arm that hard that he broke off a piece of bone and dislocated her arm. I was working down in the workshop when the boss told me to get home as soon as possible, he didn't elaborate he just said go. Turn on your headlamps and just go as fast as you can, people will get out of your way. He was right and I did that twenty miles in no time. I didn't hesitate and Sheila and the kids were in the car and we were of heading for the nearest hospital which was back in Adelaide. When we had arrived in Australia and the country having no National Health Service we had had to take out insurance to cover us for any illnesses and accidents. By the time we got to the hospital it was mayhem Juliet was screaming with pain, the other two were crying in sympathy and Sheila and I were upset to say the least. I went straight up to the counter, we need a Doctor straight away I said, the nurse barely looked up, what insurance do you have, bollocks to the insurance get a Doctor here now, I don't suffer fools lightly and this person seemed to be just that. They had to open up her arm with a six inch cut, they pinned the broken off piece of bone back into place, and she remained in Hospital for about a week. They had given us the third degree at the Hospital trying to find out what had happened, the police came and interviewed us, and later the school sent round a letter to all parents explaining what had happened, the local paper got wind of it and published the story. And then the local TV station sent someone down to interview Sheila, the interview was shown on the news that night and there was all hell to pay about this little girl being savagely beaten up on the school doorstep and no one had seen it happen. We never did find out who had done it and it left a sour taste in the mouth for quite a while. The blokes at work took the Mickey out of Sheila's accent and the fact she kept repeating that good old Brummy phrase "you know". but they were all generally pretty sympathetic towards us. The final irony was that when the Hospital bill was paid for by the Insurance Company we actually made a few dollars profit.

We were now settling in to our new rented home and our adopted country, and in the Ute I had been loaned we ranged far and near every weekend. Our nearest beach was a place called Christies Beach; the beach was at least two miles long and it had a jetty and a reef, and the most wonderful blue green warm water. When we first arrived we would spend hours on this beach. One day we met up with our Liverpudlian friends to have a Barbie, we had borrowed a bar be que plate off an Aussie mate and really felt that we had arrived, during the cooking of the steak my mate went to turn over the food and the whole lot fell into the sand, we tried to wash the sand off in the sea but it only made things worse, eating wet sandy cold steaks is not the best of ideas. Especially when you are surrounded by sniggering expert steak and sausage cooking Aussies.

We had been told about The South Australia Housing Trust, and had put our names down for a place as soon as we had got there, with Sheila pregnant and the lease being up shortly we contacted them again, due to our situation they asked us to pay them a visit. We took the kids with us up to their office just like we did to the Birmingham City Council Offices where we were ignored, made to wait for hours and treated almost like lepers, and told them that the person who had rented out the place didn't want any more children in the house. The sympathetic lady who interviewed us appeared very concerned and was tut tutting about our situation, I will write to you shortly and let you know what we are going to do. My cynical mind said to myself don't hold your breath. To prove me wrong within a week we received a letter off this kind-hearted lady telling us to be at the main garage in Christies beach two days later where we were to meet her colleague. We met the gentleman and he said I have got three properties to show you. He took us into an area called O, Sullivans Beach, which was situated on the side of a hill, the first property he took us around had views down to the sea through the huge front window, it was a three bed roomed bungalow and stood on a large piece of land. We fell in love with it immediately, after staring out of soot stained tiny windows all your life with the only view being the brick walls of the terraced houses, the brew houses, miskins and communal toilets who wouldn't have fallen for it.

On the roof of our house in Norongo Street, O,Sullivans Beach 1973.

Don't you want to see the other places he asked, no thank you this will do for us. Within a week we were in, what a contrast to our own country were we had only ever been offered one place in nine long years, and that place was at least twelve miles away from any of our families. It was an absolute credit to the Housing Trust that they treated us so kindly and didn't seem to mind that we were Poms. It was the beginning of December and we would be spending our very first Xmas away from England in our own place. We had only been here nine months, I had got a good job, the kids were in the local schools, and we felt we had landed in Paradise.

On one side of us was a true Aussie family and on the other was a family from Sweden. A couple of days after moving in Sheila went to the Aussies house to ask how she could get to the bank in Christies Beach, can I walk it or is there a bus, you cant walk that far in your condition and in this weather, the young blonde haired lady who was also pregnant said, my husband will be home shortly and he will be going to the bank so I will get him to give you a lift. Her husband came home and as promised gave Sheila lift to the bank, where do you come from he asked, England she said, well I don't like Poms he said. I found out later he had been in a partnership with a couple of Poms and being an easy going bloke they had taken advantage of him and done him out of a lot of bucks. So for Sheila it was not a very auspicious start, (when we talked about it later she called him the Pommy hater). But at the same time showing his real character he also asked her if she needed to get any shopping in, in which case he would hang around for her. We got to know this family so very well over the years; we both had young families and shared the same interests. They were golden to us and we loved them to bits, the Pommy hater and I became the very best of mates. We spent our first Xmas far away from home, in a street that appeared to be empty of people, it turned out that almost all the Aussies visit their moms and dads at Xmas time, the kids had no one to show their toys to, and cooking the turkey in the kitchen in that heat was like being in a red hot furnace, later Xmas dinners consisted of crayfish and prawns. In our new house we had a real grass front lawn, something we had never had before, one day when I had got home from work I was out on the lawn with my new hose, thumb over the end proudly sprinkling our front patch of emerald brown grass. The Pommy hater watched me from his deck chair placed on his bowling green immaculate front lawn, silly bastard he said get yourself a sprinkler, and the five-minute spray with my hose turned out to be a two-hour dousing with a proper sprinkler, and in no time ours was green too. Fancy us owning a sprinkler we felt so posh. Most of the people on our street were about our age, and being at work during the week would cut their lawns on a Sunday, this Sunday morning activity was a real community effort we found out. I was mowing my lawn with my newly acquired petrol driven mower along with a few others when I suddenly noticed that I was only person actually cutting his lawn, three or four mowers were just standing on the front lawns idling away. Intrigued I stood there looking at them when a bloke from across the road came out of his garage and gestured to me to go over, not needing any further encouragement to meet our new neighbours I went. The secret of the empty machines was revealed; the owners of the mowers were all in the garage sinking cans of the Amber Nectar. Thus I met most of our new Aussie neighbours, we expect you to take your turn with the booze one of them said, no problem was the reply.

A "Barby" in the back yard.

Sheila finally had to go into hospital at a place called McLaren Vale a place about thirty miles south from where we lived to have the baby, I had a week off work to look after the other three kids, some hopes, I was absolutely useless, I just couldn't get the knack of feeding, dressing, washing and all the things that Sheila did without me noticing. It must have been obvious to the neighbours that I was struggling because I was there one morning, with the kids undressed, unwashed and unfed and all of us unhappy when the doorbell rang, it was the heavily pregnant Pommy haters wife from next door. Out of the way she said and came straight in, right kids lets get organised. I stood by speechless as she had them all up and going and in less than ten minutes they were all washed, dressed and fed. I will be back in the morning she said. Sheila nearly died having the baby, apparently the placenta started to break up. It was at this point that things got really weird for Sheila, she was drugged up and practically unconscious when her inner being left her body and floated up towards a window, it was cold and wet outside and she started screaming for her mother, this brought the staff running in. It was a real emergency and most of the staff were involved in the panic. She told me what had happened the next morning when I went to see her and our new baby, I immediately made an appointment to see the Doctor and asked him what had happened, he tried to say it hadn't really been a problem but when I told him what she had told me and who had done and said what that night. He was amazed that we knew what had happened but put it down to the drugs, we later heard about this Out Of Body Experience thing and that made more sense. In deference to the Hospital we called the mistake Grant McLaren.

Our own Aussie child, Sheila, Grant McClaren and Graham 1971.

I was coming back from work one afternoon when I saw a barefooted, long haired guy with a full black moustache, thumbing a lift, he was dressed in a tiny pair of shorts and a white vest and being a traveller myself I naturally pulled over and he got on board, where you going, O, Sullivans Beach he said, that's where I come from I said, where abouts, Norongo Street, I live there he said what number are you at, 19, I live across the road from you. Amazing. He ended up being a mate of mine and over the years we had some epic sessions on the Amber Nectar. He had a 22-calibre air rifle and when he was under the influence he would take it out and creep round the streets shooting out the neon streetlights. If he had been caught there would have been a hefty penalty to be paid for these nocturnal activities. Later on he shot his dog and buried it in the back garden, unfortunately he hadn't buried it deep enough and during one particular hot period the dogs carcass slowly rose out of the soil feet first, it would have been funny if it hadn't have been so sad. Can you imagine it, nine months earlier we had been in snowy wintry, horrible damp conditions where the frost was on the inside of your bedroom windows, and now here I was having a drink in a real Aussie Pub, the only frost here was on the inside of my glass, the sun beating down, the beach across the road, the piss taking between the few Poms that were in there and the Aussies was right up my street, being a mans man this was heaven to me. The first time I had been asked to have a drink by an Aussie was with one of the office wallahs, he was taking me home and asked if I fancied a beer, did I ever, we went into a pub which was full of business types, there was me in my working clobber and these blokes just looked at us as we walked in and never turned a hair, no class system here then I thought. I had been a Baggies supporter prior to moving to Aussie and my Wolverhampton mate supported the Wolves. One day he said I'm going to a first division soccer match do you want to come; we were all stopping at his house for the weekend at the time in Pommy Hills, and having nothing else to do we went. We paid at the gate and the attendant said you can park over there, over there was a mound and we drove onto it, we then watched the match without having to get out of the vehicle. As it was a first Division game we were expecting a good game, these expectations were rudely shattered in the first minute, the game kicked off, the centre forward passed the ball backwards the receiver of the ball gave it an almighty boot up field, the goalie who had been taking photogenic type exercises for the benefit of the watching girls looked up just in time to see the ball bounce over his head and into the empty net. The home side got a six nil drubbing and I never went to another local soccer game after that but we did go to see the numerous British teams that played there over the years. The stopping with our Wolverhampton friends had started when we were still on the camp, they had bought a house for $11,500 dollars about £5000.00 quid, he had been a self employed painter and decorator and they had had a house to sell before they emigrated. This house, which was a bungalow, stood on a good-sized piece of land and it was everything we aspired to. We had kept in touch and we were able to invite them to the camp on Sundays for a dinner, they had to pay for it but it was cheap and quite nice. When we finally got our own place we took turns every two or three weeks at a time to stay at each others houses, eight kids and four adults, no problem.

I was telling the office wallah about the football match, he said why do you watch that silly girls game when there is real mans game of football played here right by the camp you are stopping at, he offered to pick me up take me to an Aussie rules game, naturally I accepted and that weekend I saw my first game of Aussie rules, the team were The Bays the team who's name I had seen on the walls of the Amber Nectar pub. King Kerley was revealed to be the manager of the club and was also on full view. The oval they played on was enormous, there were eighteen players on each side and each one looked hard tough and mean enough to eat you up and spit you out for breakfast. There were black and yellow flags and buntings all over the place, stalls selling the famous Aussie meat pies, and bars were you could get drinks, there was plenty of room and you could walk about freely, a bit different from one of the Baggies game I had been to on New Years day when somebody pissed down my immovable legs. I didn't know anything about the rules of this game let alone the finer points, I seemed to be the only one who saw the punch ups going on behind the play during the game, I kept asking my host why they were fighting and he telling me to shut my bloody mouth and watch the game. Despite my ignorance I really enjoyed the match and became a real fan of this hard tough Aussie game, based it was said on Gaelic Football, but with a rugby shaped ball. When I got to understand the game I began to appreciate the finer points of this rugged mans game, The skill factor was very high, to run at full pelt down a wing bounce a ball in front of you catch it then hand pass it thirty yards or kick it to one of your own players sixty or seventy yards away took some doing. And all these guys back then were amateurs, and all had full time jobs. The Aussies fans were very vociferous and to a man seemed to have a real dry sense of humour, I would go home after the games with my ribs aching from listening to the ribald comments made by the crowd. The fans would mix with each other freely and although there was plenty of good humoured banter I never in all the years I went to matches ever saw a punch up amongst these fans, it was a real family affair for some and the little kids would play just behind the small picket fence that was the only barrier between the baying fans and the players. We ended up going to every game with my Pommy hating next-door neighbour, I would take Graham and Kezia and he would take his son David. So Saturdays ended up like this, watch the kids play school football in the morning, go to the league game on the afternoon, and then watch the replays on the night, we would always sit below the score board when we were at home and could quite easily pick ourselves out at the games that were televised. The commentators on the TV were real self opinionated and not backward in giving out their views on the games. I was listening to one of them one day commentating on a live game, he said here comes little Johnny Bloggs running down the wing, I met little Johnny Bloggs on a building site one day and he was at least six feet two. As a spectacle Aussie Rules is in my opinion unsurpassed both for its ball handling skills, it's speed, and the total fearlessness of its players. There was no one prouder than me when Graham was asked to represent South Australia at Aussie rules, but that was in the future. I joined the club and was there when we won the top honour at Adelaide Cricket Oval in 1973, our colours were painted onto the top of the local breweries chimney stack which was in the middle of Adelaide as was the norm, and I also painted our house black and yellow in tribute to our side. The Pommy hater and I would go to this oval to watch the Australians hammer the Poms at cricket, again like the football games lots of comments never any trouble, we would always sit on the hill because we felt that was where the real fans sat. Because they were of similar ages Graham and David next door would play either cricket or Aussie rules constantly, these games were played outside right throughout the Summer and Winter, its no wonder the Aussies had the edge over English cricket teams when they went to Aussie, there hardly seemed to be a day when they could not practise outside. Grahams High School team won the football cup, Kerry the coach was thrown into the Onkaparinga River and much Amber Nectar was imbibed in celebration.

ON THE TOOLS.

So we had been here about eighteen months by now and everything was going great, I had a good job as a gaffer running a large contract at the Queen Elizabeth Hospital, Adelaide. My new mates had stopped calling me a Ten Pound Tourist and I was picking up the Strine. (Aussie slang) I felt we were becoming a part of our new land. One day the boss said we are going up to a place called Port Lincoln in a couple of days to have a look at a job, we will be flying there and back in one day so don't bother to pack a bag. So there I was at Adelaide Airport a couple of days later bright and early, we flew across the Spencer Gulf and the scenery was absolutely magnificent, clear blue sky, off set by the darker blue and green of the sea, we flew over the Yorke Peninsular and the tiny little islands surrounding it, what a sight and here I was getting paid for it, I was in heaven. As it turned out we missed the plane back and had to stop the night in a Hotel, I was wearing a short-sleeved shirt and shorts which in most circumstances would have been perfectly acceptable, not in this Hotel though. You cant come into this restaurant without a tie bellowed the little tubby lady Hotel owner, I haven't got one I said but we are stopping here, she said go and see the doorman he may be able to help you, I saw the doorman and he had quite a selection of ties so I knew I wasn't the first one to have been caught out, she's a real whingeing old Sheila so take your pick he said just drop it back in the morning, I picked the most expensive silk tie I could find, and it lies in my wardrobe yet. Later on that night in the restaurant while we were having dinner, a bloke staggered in, he had dusty bare feet, grimy shorts and vest and a large Aussie hat on, gimme a beer he slurred at the barman, just then the Lady Hotel owner waltzed into the room and her face was an absolute delight to see, she almost had an apoplectic purple fit there and then. How dare you come in here dressed like that she almost screamed, its easy he said I just walked through that door. You are not getting served here she cried, OK keep your bloody wig on, he said Ill go somewhere where there are real people and not two bob snobs like you, and turning on his heel he made as dignified an exit as only a man fully in his cups and his wobbly legs would allow him.

This Hospital contract was an eye-opener to me I got to understand how things were run in Aussie, and with kid gloves on was not a phrase I would use to describe their methods of telling you that something was not right. It really was in your face stuff sometimes. Our pipe work had to run from off the roof to a basement plant room, and the only route the engineers could find was down a disused plenum duct, which was about eight feet by four feet in size and was like a chimney that ran from the roof to about the second floor. There was nothing in this chimney so we had to build steel ladders and platforms to go from the bottom to the top some one hundred and twenty feet above, I would go to the yard and weld up the ladders and platforms then go back and install them Our pipes had to be brought up to the roof by the massive crane that served the site; a young guy who had a walkie-talkie controlled this crane. He would secure the load and then climb onto it holding onto the chains, this man seemed to have no fear as he was whisked up to a hundred and forty feet, generally just holding on with one hand, sun glasses on his forehead, his sun bleached corn blonde locks secured by a head band and with a cravat around his bare neck, pristine white shorts, tanned, well built and stripped to the waist he made some sight. And you could see the girls eyeing him up as he vanished skyward, the bastard. I noticed that he always swung the crane jib over the nurses home and it wasn't till I had to work in the tank room of the nurses home that I found out why, on the roof laid out on towels were numerous topless girls, when I told the lads everyone was green with envy and used to give him catcalls when he sent the crane that way, his only response being a flash of pearly white teeth on his film star handsome face and an airy wave of a sun tanned hand. One day he was to bring up a load of our pipe and not having got the balance right instead of altering the chains he just walked along the load till his weight balanced the load, and up he went one hundred and forty feet in the air just squatting on our pipes, talk about bottle.

It was inevitable that given my attitude towards authority that I would have a run in with the site foreman at the Hospital, and it wasn't long before we had an eyeball-to-eyeball confrontation, it was to do with our pipes on the roof he wanted them shifted, and when asked why he just said because, this was red rag country and after a few choice good old Anglo Saxon words, and strange Australian language the whole affair ended up with senior men from both companies deciding who was right, but with the threat of taking the pipes back down to the ground we had to back off and didn't this rankle. At least it cleared the air and we both treated each other with a grudging respect after that. Later on during the contract he told me he had been in on the Saturday to inspect a third story roof, he had got a clearance pass and had gone onto the ward and opened the window to climb out onto the roof to have a look, when suddenly he found himself dragged back into the corridor where he was wrestled to the ground by three burly porters and dragged away into an office. The fight for that's what it turned out to be lasted about five minutes till he managed to tell them who he was and what he was doing. It turned out that the area he was in was the psychiatric ward and the porters thought he was a demented madman trying to commit suicide by throwing himself out of the window. I don't think he was too impressed when I said I thought he was too. There was a lift company on the site installing lifts in the new block, their safety arrangements seemed to be absolutely water tight, every floor had a boarded off lockable area outside the lift area, and when these doors were open there was always a man stood there to stop anyone going near. There was a man in the lift room at the top who would control the lift by an electric hand winch, and would only move it under orders from the man in the cradle suspended below him. These blokes were a cheerful lot and especially an Italian guy who was always singing. As we passed them when they were having their Smoko I used to pretend to be their boss and would tell them to get off their arses and back to it. One day in mid morning there was a lot of shouting and noise going on, it seemed there had been an accident on site, building site workers are generally a close knit lot and tend to look after their own, and this site was no different. The rumpus was coming from the seventh floor, which was one below us so we ran to see if we could help, the lift lads were there and the one who controlled the winch was crying inconsolably, what's going off someone asked, one of our lads has fallen out of the cradle from this floor was the grim reply. It turned out to be the singing Italian. Within an hour the place was awash with police and safety officers, you didn't see safety officers on sites so much then, and they came in for some real stick. The results of which was a mass influx of inspectors whose reports cost the main contractor a small fortune to implement, serves them right was the general consensus. It was concluded by the inquest, that the safety procedures applied by the company had been one hundred percent. What had happened was that the Italian had been using some gas cutting equipment to remove existing bolts from the lift shaft walls, he had entered the lift shaft on the tenth floor where the bottles were correctly strapped in a bottle truck which was standing in the locked area on the floor. As he proceeded down the shaft he would rest the hoses over the handrail of the cradle, it seems that when he picked up the gun the next time he picked it up from underneath the rail thus completing a loop around the rail, as the cradle went downwards so it slowly pulled the bottles over the edge of the lift shaft and they fell in and knocked him through the small gap between the cradle and the lift shaft wall, he fell right to the bottom of the lift shaft and was instantly killed. The atmosphere on site was terrible for quite some time after this incident and everyone became a little more safety conscious. It is a little known fact but building sites are the most dangerous of places to work. and have more fatalities than any other industry including miners, and when one of your own kind gets killed or injured and although you may not have known him well a black cloud descends on the site and it's almost like losing a relative.

The first day that we had gone on site at the Hospital I had pulled up at the raised barrier to be confronted by a guy who was dressed like an SS Storm trooper, he had on black leather calf length boots, a pair of black Jodhpurs, a gleaming white jacket with a highly polished black leather belt around his waist and topped off by a shiny peaked black cap complete with silver badge, the only thing missing it seemed was the standard Luger gun. He really looked and acted the part and I knew instinctively that he and I were going to have fun. He stood menacingly black leathered hand in a stopping gesture in front of the van, he had obviously taken an instant dislike to me, you cannot come in here he said in guttural accent, we have come here to start work on the new building I said moving forward, he backed off slightly as he tried once more to stop me going in but I said if you don't move Ill drive over your shiny F***ing boots. I cant stand people who when they get a couple of stripes have a go at their own kind and this bloke was a prime example of why. He finally got the message and reluctantly got out of the way when I inched forward; I parked by the other builders vans in our allocated area and thought nothing more of it. Several days later we had taken an amount of gear into one of the loading bays but when we got back to the van after about an hour and drove off we found had got two punctures, I looked at the back tyres and there in each one was a three cornered steel jack. I knew who had done it and decided to get him back. It took me three days to find out where the SS man parked his car and when I did I returned his jacks. The following day he glowered as he let us in but we never had any more trouble off the SS man. A couple of months later and with the ladders and platforms installed down the chimney it was time to lower the ten inch diameter steel pipes, along with the smaller thirty foot long four inch pipes down the shaft. The builder had put a mobile crane on the roof and had supplied a man to control it, in view of the accident no one was taking safety lightly. Because the shaft was so small only one person at a time could be in there when the pipes were lowered, and that person was me. Over a hundred feet above me I had my mate in the shaft in contact with the crane man, I had a whistle around my neck tied on a piece of tatty string I had found, and the signals were, one blast for down, two blasts for up and three for stop. The first four pipes went in like clockwork, although it took a long time to install them, so much so that the site foreman said any monkey can control that crane and promptly took his man off elsewhere. We had got the next two large pipes in position and they were lowering a smaller sized one when it caught on one of the brackets about twenty feet above my head, my intention was to blow three times for the pipe to be stopped but on the second blow the string broke and the whistle flew out of my hand and down thirty foot into the gloom. Apart from being a nuisance I didn't think it too much of a problem and started to climb down to retrieve the whistle. What I hadn't realised was that the man above me had heard the signal of two blasts and so had given the order to the man on the roof who had started to raise the pipe. I got to the bottom of the eight foot by four foot chamber and scrabbling around I finally found the whistle. It was at this point when I was about to climb the ladder that I heard an almighty bang, and looking up one hundred and twenty feet was absolutely horrified to see the lights being ripped out as the pipe dropped like an express train, the noise was awful. Fear is a wonderful thing it certainly concentrates your mind, I must only have had seconds to decide what to do, in the wall was a two foot square exit duct, I'll go through there I thought, this was immediately discounted because with my body flat I would be exposing more of myself than if I was stood up. A death defying decision and so it was I just stood with my back to the duct wall relied on my crap luck and hard hat and shouted. There was an ear-shattering bang as the thirty foot long pipe hit the concrete floor, the whole shaft went pitch black and lights cables and debris showered down on me for what seemed an eternity. When the debris had stopped falling I felt around for the offending pipe and there it was no more than six inches from my body. I became aware of my young mate high above me screaming my name, he and everyone else on the roof really had thought I had been killed. I waited for a moment or two in the silent black darkness of what could have been my coffin and then shouted back up to him and said can you send the next one down a little bit slower. He was immediately physically sick and was shaking so much I had to send him home in a taxi. The site foreman tried to deny he had taken his man off us but there was no getting away with this. The pipe had gone right to the top when it had caught under a bracket, the one inch hemp rope had broken under the strain and down came the pipe it had gone right through the six inch concrete floor, it had landed smack in the middle of an electrical cable tray and cut as neat a circle as you would wish through the main cables to the operating theatres, luckily back up generators had started instantly so there was no problem there. When I spoke to the electrician later he said if that pipe hadn't jumped out of the cut in the cables you could have been fried to death if you had touched it. The site foreman came in for some real stick, I said to him a monkey might be able to operate the crane but obviously an Aussie couldn't. When people asked me how I felt about the incident I told them I felt quite safe because I was wearing a safety helmet. That night there was much Amber Nectar sunk to celebrate my near miss.

On the roof of the Queen Elizabeth Hospital, Adelaide. Before going for a liquid lunch. 1972.

This as it turned out was only the first of two or three death defying incidents. There were no further incidents with pipes until we reached the second floor, the pipe work bracketed to the ceiling was to run the full length of a corridor and this corridor ran for about two hundred feet, the brickies were building a wall along the complete length of this area, they had got to the full height all along and were putting the finishing touches to it, we were on one side of the wall and they were on the other, we were welding lengths of pipes together in preparation to lifting them into their brackets, it was a wet and very windy cold day and working in this corridor was like being in a wind tunnel so I said to my mate who came from Leicester lets get down to Smoko early so as to get a warm, we had only gone about twenty feet and down half a flight of stairs when there was a huge deafening crash, we raced back upstairs to find the wall had collapsed along half of its full length burying our pipe work and equipment below tons of bricks, the brickies and their labourers were frantically tearing at this mound of rubble shouting where were they, we started to help these panic stricken blokes, who we looking for said my mate, two pipe fitters was the reply, they were here a minute ago and now we cant hear them. You silly bastards that's us, they were so relieved they hadn't killed us they couldn't even abuse us in reply.

We had really begun to settle in now, the three kids were all at local schools and the mistake was at a part time nursery. Sheila had got herself a little part time job and everything seemed to be going our way. When she walked the kids to school what she couldn't figure out was how the men on the road seemed to know her name, she would get wolf whistles and shouts of G, day Sheila from some of the passing blokes. I had to explain to her that the Aussies called all the females Sheila; it was just like us calling them love.

After returning from the liquid lunch.

Things though were not all as rosy as that, when I had agreed to run the biggest contract my boss had ever had I had laid down a couple of stipulations, one was that I got everything I ordered as soon as possible and the second was that I had no office intervention as to how I ran this contract save of course money and contractual matters. I had been in charge of this job without any interference from the office for about eighteen months and we were in front of programme and there was only about two months left on site. It was then that for some reason my boss who had been like a father to us and to who I owed almost everything started to get himself involved in the contract, I took this personally as a slight against myself and made my views known in no uncertain terms. The upshot was a visit one day from my football loving mate, one look at his face was enough to tell me what was about to happen, you've come here to give me the bullet haven't you, he hesitated and then said yes, I dropped the piece of pipe I was carrying onto the floor, Ill be off then. Hang on he said aren't you going to tell me what's to do to finish the contract, you are taking the piss was my reply, see you later, and I was gone. I got a job with another local company but the money was nowhere near what I had been earning. Things looked a little bleak for a while, although I got on well with office wallahs and workmates, and then after about six weeks I had a phone call off my old boss, can I come and see you he asked, I knew immediately he was in trouble at the Hospital, I had a lot respect for this man, he had helped us when we were down and had looked after us as if we were part of his family, sure I said call in on Sunday. When he came and sat at our table I think he found it difficult to ask me to go back, but he had brought on the situation and it was time to be hard nosed and I was in no mind to help him. He eventually got around to asking me to go back to him, I saw Sheila behind him waving her arms and nodding a frantic yes, I will think about it I said I am quite happy where I am. He frowned, I was prepared to offer you another dollar an hour if you do come back. I told him I would think about it and ring him later on during the week. I gave in my notice the next day and rang my old boss up on the Thursday, OK Ill start back with you. Monday I went back to the Hospital and picked up the very same piece of pipe I had thrown down six weeks earlier. And after this incident of course things were never really the same.

CRABBING.

The Pommy hater from next door stuck his head over the fence one day, ever been crabbing he asked, nope, well how about coming with us this Saturday and Ill show you what it is all about. I never needed two invites to do anything and asked what time to be ready, Ill check the tides and let you know, check the tides? Blimey what had I agreed to?

My mate said can you get hold of some chicken wire and a couple of broom stales. I managed to get some wire off the job I was on and bought two broom stales, He came around the next night and told me what he wanted me to make, we fashioned rings about twelve inches in diameter out of light re-enforcing wire these rings where attached to the broom stales and opposite the broom stale we had fashioned a three inch spike, the tennis bats because that's what they looked like were then covered in the chicken wire. I was intrigued, how can you catch crabs with a tennis bat, the Pommy hater didn't reply he just looked smug. We set out with our families in tow on the Saturday, its about seventy miles he had told us so bring plenty of drinks and eats it can be a long hot day. We finally arrived at a place called St Kilda, and parked up in the sand dunes, before us stretched a vast expanse of beach, the sea in the Gulf of St Vincent was nowhere to be seen, the sun was belting down and to say the least it was hot. We rigged up covers for the families between the side of the cars, my mate looked at his watch, we go in twenty minutes he said, where I asked looking around at the empty sky and beach, there he said pointing out to where I presumed the sea lay. Two further pieces of equipment were unloaded from his vehicle these were two, three feet diameter round copper tank bottoms about eighteen inches deep and each had a string attached to it. Again I was mystified as to what all this strange looking gear meant, how do you catch crabs with a five-foot tennis bat and half of a large can? We set off under the blazing sun, my mate and David, me and Graham, the half cans we rolled along and the kids carried the tennis bats, we walked out what must have been two miles in that unforgiving Sun. My mate looked at his watch again, won't be long now he said. By now we could see little rollers approaching us as the tide began to come in, we waited, when the sea was about a foot deep he flipped the cans onto the water where they floated, he tied the string around his waist and I did the same, lets go he said, as he slowly backed towards the distant beach, where's the bloody crabs I almost screamed, just watch and do as I do was the enigmatic reply, I watched him wait till the sea was about knee depth, suddenly the tennis bat shot into the water and emerged with a big blue crab clutching the wire, he expertly flipped it over his shoulder where it landed in the can, I was amazed. He said look for shadows as they come towards you, when they rear up at you shove the tennis bat at them, they will attack the bat and all you have to do is sling it into the can, it don't matter if they drop a leg or two there will be plenty for all of us. If they don't grab the wire then stick them with the spike on the front of the bat. I certainly hadn't realized how fast crabs can move in their own environment. Suddenly the Pommy hater leapt into the air turning it blue with the most awful language, for a split second I felt momentarily concerned until I saw the big blue crab hanging on his naked big toe. I was in absolute bits and found it hard not to take the piss out of him, is this the Aussie way of crabbing using yourself as bait I asked him. We walked and he limped backwards to the beach and long before we had got there we had at least a hundred large blue crabs in the cans, we put the cans in the back of his vehicle and he went and got some seawater and put it over the crabs. We will have to stop at Christies on the way back for some fresh seawater for cooking them in he said. By the time we had got back home it was about nine o'clock at night, everybody was hot and thirsty and hungry. We had collected a few gallons of fresh seawater from the beach and the Pommy hater produced a huge saucepan that held at least two gallons, we set it on the gas rings to boil. Finally when it was boiling he threw in loads of crabs, give them five minutes he said then we can get stuck in. Was there ever a better meal than this, fresh hot crab and plenty of it washed down with cans of the ice cold Amber Nectar, sitting outside in the warm black night, superb, magnificent, wonderful, and all done by our very own hands. There was much eating and drinking that night and it was brilliant. I love sea food and when I went into a Deli for the first time I was amazed to see king sized prawns on sale for 50 cents a carton, I had prawns for breakfast dinner and took home some for tea. Lobster was as cheap as chips and we had many a seafood meal with lobster and prawns and salad, wonderful fare on a warm Aussie night. The Pommy hater was great at getting any food that was going for free, and down by a place called Port Stanvac where the oil tankers came in there was a rocky cove, this was the original O,Sullivans Beach, and on the rocks could be seen the outline of a hut or house that had been built there years and years ago, it made you wonder what sort of life these original settlers had, hard and tough I would have thought. He took us there one day armed with buckets, and there amongst the rocks were thousands of peri-winkles, and these were big ones, the last time I had seen peri-winkles was when my mom used to buy them for a tanner a pint off the bloke who used to come around Summer Lane on a Sunday afternoons. She loved them and would have been in her oil tot here. It was great just take them home, boil them up and away you went.

The "Mudlarks" Debbie and Grant in the pool outside our house 1973.

In the road where we lived at the back of the houses across the road there was a creek, this held a lot of attraction for the kids especially in the summer for swimming in, I was there with the kids one day when I noticed a lad with a bamboo stick, a piece of string was tied on the end and attached to that was a small piece of meat, he lowered it into the water and waited a couple of minutes then very slowly and carefully he raised the bait out of the water and hanging there by a large claw was a miniature lobster, I was amazed what's that called I asked him, it's a Yabbie he said looking at me a little strangely, what will you do with it, eat it he said and went back to his stealthy game, naturally at the first opportunity we were there having a go, and although they were small and a little bit finicky to get at, they were tasty and free.

UP THE BUSH.

I want you to fly to Whyalla said the boss one day; you are going to meet an engineer at the airport and then drive up to a place called Ceduna. I eagerly looked up Ceduna on the map; it was a place about four hundred and sixty kilometres from Whyalla. I was chuffed I was actually going to see the real bush close up. I caught the seven oclock morning flight from Adelaide Airport and met the engineer on time in Whyalla, Ill drive the first one hundred miles he said and you can drive the next one hundred is that OK, it certainly is. We took off in a big American estate car, we left Whyalla behind and he really put his foot down, we were doing about one hundred and ten miles an hour but because there was nothing to judge the speed by we just seemed to be dawdling. The bush or as the Aussies call it the Mulga consisted of bushes scrub and trees as far as the eye could see, we were on a long straight road that disappeared into the distance like a black ribbon placed on the landscape. If I didn't realise before then this trip showed me just how vast this country was, when the road rose above the surrounding bush you could see for miles, and what you could see for miles was just the Mulga, we ploughed on through the bush when after about fifty five minutes he pulled over, your turn he said, blimey have we covered a hundred miles already. I took over the wheel and flattened the accelerator, about fifty minutes later he said can you see those silos up front, and there on the horizon were some huge two hundred foot high grain silos, we will pull in there for a break, and take it easy when you get there, take it easy who did he think he was talking to, I considered myself an excellent driver so pressed on regardless. The turn off to the little town appeared on the right, don't try to turn said the engineer through clenched teeth, why not I asked, look at your speed he said, I glanced down, eighty miles an hour read the clock, we shot right past the turning and I had to sheepishly turn round and go back. When we got to Ceduna we had to have a look at putting air conditioning at the local cop shop, we got there and stepped around the drunken Aboriginals, who even at this early hour were strewn on the pavement outside the nick. I asked the cop behind the desk why they were allowed to lie there, we don't nick them for being pissed anymore he said, we have virtually abandoned the offence. I got to talking to the cops in the station and asked them how big their beat was, we go five hundred kilometres up to the Western Australia border and then inland for about a thousand kilometres and then back here, we stay out two or three nights depending on what happens. Blimey it made the normal coppers beat around Aston look like a Sunday morning stroll. It certainly was a different life when you got out of the cities. We stayed that night in the local Hotel. Can you play cribbage the engineer asked, I certainly can, he challenged me to play, I must warn you he said I was our club champ for two years on the trot, Ho Hum, when he was four games down he started to get serious, and wouldn't let me or the barman leave until he had squared things up, I think his cunning plan was to get me drunk and I had to play really well to lose to him it was a long long night, but he wasn't going to lose out to a Pom.

One day the boss asked me if I was prepared to work away from home, certainly I said, its at a place called Tumby Bay, its by Port Lincoln on the Lincoln Highway and it's a bit of a drive, the bit of a drive turned out to be a twelve hour slog through the heat of the day, the road hugging the coast around the Gulf of Saint Vincent and down the Eyre Peninsula towards the Southern Ocean. I was driving a company lorry loaded with all sorts of materials, pipes, benches, tools, bracketing and a host of other things. We were going to be working at a hospital. I have fixed up your rooms at the local Hotel the boss had told me. This was a first for me, whenever I had been away from home before, it was sort out your own digs and grub and just carry on. I found out that when you worked away from home in Aussie, you weren't expected to out of pocket in any shape or form. They made provision to do your laundry, and in some cases you were allowed the first two drinks free in the bar. This was a lot different from living out of a suitcase on a diet of chips and pints. Which just goes to show what a decent Union could do for its members if its Officers did their jobs properly instead of playing the politics game. It was late in the day when we got to Tumby Bay and I was tired so we went to the Hotel, which turned out to be the local pub and booked in. This was when I found out that every pub had to be able to put up bona-fide travellers, and all pubs were called Hotels. A night in the bar and the next day we went to the hospital to start our contract. Who are you mate asked the head porter, we have come to do the air-conditioning, and the plumbing I said, hang on a bit Ill get hold of the builder. After about an hour the builder rolled up, can I help he asked, yes we are here to start installing the services, well you'll be lucky mate he said we aint even started the footings yet, but she'll be apples, I was non-plussed, she'll be apples what could this mean, he means it will be alright my Aussie mate whispered. Someone somewhere had got crossed wires and we weren't due to start for at least another six weeks. We wearily unloaded the materials into a shed and set off on the long journey back home. When we finally got back on the job two months later there was enough of the building up for us to start. I was working up the bush , and I had a young lad of sixteen with me, we were staying at the local Hotel as usual. Breakfast consisted of bacon, eggs, tomatoes and big lamb chops, lamb chops for breakfast, who would ever believe it. The lad I had with me was an Aussie rules football player and although he was only sixteen he towered over me, and he was also as thin as a lath. One day the chef walked through the dining room, he was from Manchester and stopped to have a rattle, what was a bloke from Manchester doing in this little flyspeck on the map place, I never asked and he never offered so never found out. Blimey your thin he said looking at my beanpole mate tutt tutting, Ill give you a steak tonight and I want you to eat it all up. I think my skinny mate brought out the mothering instinct in him. That night he came over to our table with the biggest piece of meat I have ever seen in my life, get that into you lad he said, and my lean mate obliged. This kid was amazing he would eat anything like a starving ostrich but he was a growing lad and had a big frame to fill out. After that he got all the best meat and food but he never put on an ounce. We were sitting outside the back of the Hotel one warm summers night listening to the Ocean lapping up the beach, drinking the Amber Nectar, the vast night sky was as black as velvet, it was that dark you couldn't see the person sitting next to you and the millions of stars that surrounded us from the horizon all around twinkled and shone like diamonds, they looked as if you could put your hand in the air and pluck them down. Shooting stars occasionally swept towards earth and vanished in bright lines that stayed on impressed on your eyeballs for some little time after. I had never experienced a night like this before and it was wonderful.

In the Hotel at night time the locals played pool, and the losers had to buy tickets from behind the bar which if you were lucky you could win two three four six or a dozen bottles of beer. I was pretty good at pool and despite being a whinging no hoper ten pound tourist Pom after about a week they all wanted me as a partner. When I drove home after staying there six weeks I had about six dozen clinking bottles of beer on board. One night one of the locals said do you want to go to my brother's stag night, OK I said where is it going to be, they weren't spoilt for choice in this little place, just the pub and the Yacht Club. It's going to be held in a sheep Shearer's shed, bloody hell what next, it will cost you five bucks each to pay for the booze, how do we get there I asked, easy he said and took me outside, there it is he said pointing to a shack on the side of the hill in the distance, just go down the Lincoln Highway and turn into the gate. On the night me and my mate got into the truck and drove over to the party, the shed was full of Aussies hitting the Amber Nectar big time, and I needed no second offer to join them. The booze was on the table where the Shearer's would throw the wool when they had shorn the sheep. Behind the table was a slope that led to the dips, where when they had given the sheep a haircut they would just kick them up the backside and down the ramp they would go into the dip. During this wild night of drinking huge amounts of the Amber Nectar there were quite a few blokes who found out just what it was like to go down this ramp. Where do you go for a piss, I asked a bloke, just go to the doorway and let loose he said. I did as he said and was enjoying a good P when I heard a shout from down below, the doorway was up a flight of stairs that had no handrail and some unlucky sod had fallen down the five foot or so distance and being too drunk to move had just lain there getting peed on by all and sundry. I do not remember driving home from what commonly became known as the Sheep Shearer's Ball. I do remember getting up the next day with a raging headache to find the truck parked right in the middle of the square outside the pub. When I got into it to park properly I noticed some scratch marks on the windscreen, where had they come from, I got out and inspected the truck front, there were parallel scratches up and over the bonnet, who did that I wondered. My mate provided the answer, when you said you had had enough you got into the truck, flew through the parked cars like a racing driver without touching anything and went off down the dirt track like a bloody madman, I told you to stop at the main road but you just drove straight across it and through the barbed wire fence on the other side you chucked a "U" and came straight back out again. I just had to see if he was right and drove the couple of miles to have a look, and fair enough there opposite the dirt track road was a gap in the barbed wire fence and in the paddock was a perfect circle of tyre tracks going round and coming back out of the same hole. Blimey what was this Amber Nectar stuff? To try and disguise the scratches on the truck we started feeding by hand out of the windows the huge Pacific gulls chips at dinner time, the plan was for them to cover the scratches with bird shit. It must have worked because no one ever asked where the marks had come from.

We would have Sundays off and I would take the truck and just pick a road to go along, my mate would have his rifle poking out of the window shooting at the crows or anything else that moved, one day he actually bagged two of these elusive black scavengers, one on the ground and one in full flight, it was that good a shot it just had to be luck. I finally got fed up of him having all the fun so I taught him to drive and then it was my turn for some shooting. We were going down a country road one day when we saw a sign that said "Nowhere Else" twenty three miles, being nosy I backed up and down the track we went, exactly twenty three miles later Nowhere Else was revealed to be the end of a disused railway track where they would load up the sheep for transport to Adelaide and various other towns in the area in days gone by. So much for being nosy. We ranged far and near over the Eyre Peninsula, from Port Lincoln to Streaky Bay, and to Coffin Bay where Captain Cook had apparently lost some coffins over board some two hundred years before, wonderful wild places with a natural ruggedness that pleased the eye. After three weeks of hard graft I decided we deserved a day off so we went to Port Lincoln to do some fishing, we rented a small boat and I asked the bloke where a good spot was for fishing, there he said pointing across the huge bay, is there enough juice in this thing to get us there and back? There's enough diesel in there to get you to Adelaide he said. Good enough and off we went. It took us ages to get across this bay, what I didn't realise at the time is that this bay was the apparently the second largest in the world, only Rio de Janeiro being bigger, also the great white shark was as common as chips in this area. We spent the day catching sea salmon, and like fools just threw them in the bottom of the boat, when they curled up and started to smell we turfed them over board. Finally we set sail across the bay, my mate was captain and I was just lying back admiring the blue skies, it was while I was looking up that I suddenly saw my feet appear above my head Id had some experience of this rolling action whilst this sailing here so I knew what it meant, I sat up rapidly, to be confronted by rolling waves at least ten foot high, the tide was on the move and we were going up and down in the troughs, one minute you could see land, the next minute you were down in a watery hole the engine screaming as the propeller cleared the water on the crest of the waves. I am no great swimmer and there being no lifebelts on board ship so I thought that discretion was better part of valour in this instance so I turned round to my mate who was just lying back completely oblivious to what I saw as a mortal peril. Turn right and head for the shore I said trying not to scream at him and frighten him, why, look at the bloody waves I said, Oh yeh, just get moving. We slowly wended our way back to the shoreline and hugged the coast until we got back to the boat hirer, so much for pinching days off, but it was an experience I wouldn't have wanted to miss.

SETTLING IN.

We had been in our house a couple of years now and had settled in quite well with the local Aussies, because they mostly went away at Xmas we had decided to invite them all to our house on our wedding anniversary which was the twenty fifth of March. Getting drinks for the party was no problem in Aussie, you just drove down to the local pub and into the drive through, hard working bar staff asked you what you wanted and that amount of beer and drinks was placed onto the back seat of your car and off you went in no time, one of the bar staff was a neighbour of ours from the other end of the street and he always looked after us. We had a great night and this event was repeated till the year we left. Sheila would make a punch for these party's and with the stuff she put in it it was pretty potent. One of our neighbours from across the road was a real teetotaller and would never let alcohol pass his lips, during the party he asked for a soft drink and Sheila without thinking about it said why don't you try some of this punch, he drank a glass and soon came back for more, that's great he said, within ten minutes this quiet unassuming man was dancing like a dervish his hair flying wildly all over the place, and he came over the next day and said that was the best night he had had in years. Sheila hadn't got the heart to tell him he had been lashing down, gin, rum, vodka, and various other potent mixtures of booze. I had heard on the local radio an Aussie actor named Chips Rafferty recite a poem called "The man from Snowy River" written by Banjo Patterson and I was really taken with this poem, which seemed to me to embody all that was good about Australia and its inhabitants. Hard tough straight talking people. I decided to learn it, and for the next six months I sent Sheila and the kids mad as I drove around listening to a tape of the poem, as I tried to get my head around its thirteen long verses. I finally did it and on the night of our party for our wedding anniversary I duly recited it word perfect, if I expected cheering or applause I was sadly mistaken, sit down you silly bastard was the Pommy haters comment as people began to yawn and show signs of wanting to escape this mad Englishman's ranting, although some of the more refined people there later said well done. Even to this day I can recite huge chunks of that poem, but not in front of Sheila or the kids, it had made that much of an impression on me. Both our girls had by now joined the local Brownies group, and we were expected to support them in every way we could, one night they put on a show at a place called Strathalbyn which was a little town about fifty miles from where we lived, we got to the village hall and it was like being transported back to the thirties, some of the older ladies had fox wraps around their necks, and the local scout master was resplendent in full uniform and tight shorts, making a thorough prat of himself, the boy scouts and the girls sang and did their pieces and both the Vicar and the scoutmaster ran true to form by making fools of themselves, I laughed that much my sides ached for quite a while. When we came out of the hall I was surprised to see a light frost on the windscreen of the car, I just hadn't expected to see the stuff, and the cold had a sharp bite to it, but we were up in the hills, and I was assured it was quite usual for this time of the year.

My new next door mate asked me if Id ever been rabbit shooting, no, well if you get yourself a gun I will take you sometime, I finally went to the local sports shop and bought myself a two point two rifle, I took it to the local cop shop for it to be registered, is it loaded asked the copper on the desk, I don't know I said feeling foolish, he took it out of its cardboard box and expertly checked it over. I gave my name, and address and he handed over the gun, with what I thought was a small look of misgiving, but he did say happy hunting and I left the Station with a weapon that could kill a man a quarter of a mile away, it was as easy as that. Now that you have a gun the Pommy hater said have you sorted out the sights yet? Sorted out the sights, don't you just put them on the gun and that's it? No way here in Aussie we do things right, and not wanting to look stupid I went along with what he said, I've got a mate who has a property not too far away Ill arrange for us to go there and set the gun up. We got to his mates place, I've got a Pom here who wants to set up a rifle you got anywhere he can do it he asked, yep I know just the place he replied giving my mate a what I can only term as an old fashioned look, follow me. We went about a hundred yards from his house, we got to a clearing, here's a good spot he said, he took out a small piece of paper and walked about fifty feet away and stuck it to a tree, get down on that mound there he said and let fly, I looked around and there was what seemed to be the perfect man made spot for lying down and shooting. How professional I thought they must have done this lots of times before I, how many guns do these blokes own. The property owner and my mate both stamped their feet and gingerly backed away from me, what's the matter with them I thought do they think I'm going to shoot them? Excitedly I took aim Ill show these Aussies what a real Englishman can do, I took a shot, you missed the tree you dingbat, have another go, I wriggled to get a firmer position, I squinted down the sights when I saw something moving towards me along the barrel, I sat up suddenly feeling very itchy and then realised with rising horror that the man made hill I was sitting on was in fact an ant hill and these three quarter inch long black ants with large nippers were certainly not pleased to see me there. I leapt about six feet in the air and began to frantically brush off what seemed like an army of ants, I turned to my mates help me I said, this plea fell on deaf ears as both of them were yards away from me and bent over with laughter. When I had finally got rid of the ants I saw the joke and the Aussies shook my hand for taking it in good part. We went to the property owners shed and he put the gun in a vice aiming at a piece of white paper stuck to a lump of wood, just fire at that, I did so now line up the sights on the bullet hole, I adjusted the sights to suit, there you are he said, easy. I was grateful for the advice but not for the bites.

Some months later, there's a moonless night coming up so its about time we went rabbi ting said my next door mate, Ill arrange for us to go down east for a bit of shooting, so there we were one Saturday afternoon heading east in his mates pickup Ute, on the back was a metal framework and attached to this was a tyre bolted flat down about four feet high, what's that for I asked, you'll find out when we get there was the only reply I could get out of either of them. Where are we going to be shooting, we will know when we get there. We had driven about a hundred and fifty miles when my mate said try this one, this one turned out to be the entrance to a farming property. We drove the mile or so to the typical low-slung canopied farmhouse, the Cocky came out, Gday mate any chance of shooting on your paddocks, sure was the laconic reply, go down there to the lower paddock and try not to shoot any of my sheep. With that he vanished and so did we. We had to wait till dark and while we were waiting the secret of the tyre was revealed, when we get going there will be one bloke on the spotlight, one bloke driving and the other bloke stood on the back of the pickup in the tyre. He will be doing the shooting. Dusk finally came and then complete darkness, as predicted there was no moon, we sat there waiting until my mate said OK lets give it a go. The engine was started but instead of putting on the headlamps a powerful spotlight attached to the roof was lit up; it had a narrow beam and could swivel at any angle. Because I was the learner I was told to drive and when the bloke on the lamp said stop I had to stop. Easy I thought, as it was to prove it was in fact very difficult, we took off slowly naturally I tended to follow the lamp but as this was shining all over place it was a fairly hard thing to do, don't follow the lamp said the searchlight operator just go straight ahead, what happens if I run into something, run into something, what's to run into in the middle of a three mile square paddock? Miffed by the logic of his retort I drove straight ahead, stop my companion hissed, I slowly came to a halt can you see it he asked the shooter in the back, I see it was the reply, a crack and a shout of got it, he jumped off the back and ran about thirty yards in front of the pickup, bent down and picked up the inert body of a rabbit. It was all done so quickly I hadn't seen a thing. He slung the carcass into the back of the pickup, and during the night it was followed by at least fifty more. One part I didn't like was that if you hadn't killed the rabbit outright to put it out of its misery you would have to stand on its head and pull its back legs upwards till its neck broke. I had a go on the lamp and was finally let onto the back with my gun, I only shot a couple of rabbits on this trip but I improved as we went on more outings. Rabbits are strange animals I found out, when they were caught in the spotlight they would sink down to the ground and freeze, because it was a moonless night the spotlight was the only thing to be seen, the crouching rabbit was almost invisible, how's he going to shoot that I whispered, just watch and listen was the reply, from the back of the pickup came a long low whistle, I watched the rabbit fascinated, slowly it raised its ears, another low whistle and the rabbit began to sit up, once more and the rabbit was up and in full view, crack and down it went in a heap. We stayed on that one paddock all that night and when the pink dawn came it was time to pack up, in the back of the pickup the bodies were piled in a bloody heap, what we going to do with them I asked, skin and gut them was the reply. My mate got out his knife and expertly slit the rabbit from crotch to its neck, he opened up its stomach and with a long practised movement removed the guts without even touching them. I was impressed, impressed that is till I got a whiff of the guts and blood, I went round the front of the pickup and spewed up, you OK, yes Ill manage I said. I was to go on lots more shoots in the future but this first trip was a real eye-opener. As for the rabbits the ones we didn't have in stews were kept in the deep freezer and were got rid on crabbing trips when we used the nets.

We had finally saved up enough money to go on a holiday, when I had worked in Tumby Bay I had noticed a small holiday type place with chalets, a small nine hole golf course, and was close to a jetty. I rang them up and booked us in for two weeks, we loaded up the estate wagon and trailer with our little crew on board and took off. I drove most of the way until we got past Whyalla, then Sheila took the wheel, she hadn't been behind the wheel for more than ten minutes when we had a puncture, and with the load we had on board and the trailer things got a little hairy for a while as she fought with the wheel as we slewed all over the road, luckily it was quiet so there was no real danger. I had to take the trailer off and unload the back of the car to get at the spare tyre, which was a real pain. We set sail again and after about an hour as we drove down the Lincoln Highway we saw on the horizon what we thought was a rain cloud, as we drove towards it it seemed to be moving in a strange way. The sky suddenly went dark and we found ourselves in the middle of a massive locust swarm, there were literally millions of the things, and they began to smash into the car from every angle, the kids were screaming and I wasn't too happy either, what shall I do asked Sheila, just carry on I said. Large mistake, in no time at all the locusts had completely covered the car and more importantly the radiator and we could smell the things cooking as they blocked it up. The car ground to a halt with the radiator boiling over, so there we sat motionless, the car covered in two inch long locusts, the windscreen was just one big smear, and with the smell of frying bodies in our nostrils, our first holiday was off to a pretty bad start. The inside of the car was red hot with the heat and we couldn't open the windows. We sat there for what seemed hours but was only probably only minutes for the massive cloud to pass over us. Eventually the swarm had gone, luckily we had plenty of water on board and it took ages to get the cooked bodies out of the radiator and the engine compartment and we were on our way once again. As usual we ranged far and near on this holiday visiting some really remote, rugged places. We went to Port Lincoln one day and took a ride on a little boat to a small island, this trip was organised by the Cocky no doubt to earn extra money, we got to the island and he drove us around doing a bit of site seeing, although there wasn't that much to see. Finally he took us to a place called Squeaky Beach, this name became immediately obvious when you walked on the pure white sands, it was fantastically soft and it literally squeaked as you walked on it with bare feet. What a place and what a beach.

A CHANGE OF JOBS.

Although I thought the world of him because of the way he had helped us, relations with my first boss had not improved, I put this squarely down to myself and the chip on my shoulder regarding authority figures. I was earning good money but was not really happy with my work life. It was during this period that I had a phone call off the manager of the mechanical services department of the company whom I had spent six weeks with after an earlier incident. Can I come and see you he asked, of course I said intrigued. He came over that Sunday, I have got to fill a position in my section of Supervisor, he will be my right hand man and because of the way you performed when you were with us I would like to offer it to you. He had me on the hook instantly I had only done six weeks for them and here he was offering me an office position. How much does it pay, it turned out that it was quite a lot less than I was earning at the moment and not only that but there would be a three month probationary period, so if I didn't measure up I could be thrown out on my ear. Can I think about it please, yes but I want the position filled as soon as possible. All that night Sheila and I discussed the offer, on the one hand it was less money but on the other it was a real step up the ladder for me, and if I did well an office job was certainly more secure than contracting. We decided we would go for it, and so after a week I found myself working in a very busy office. It was a whole new world to me, I was taught how to estimate, how to order materials, go to site meetings, all the things I never thought I would have a chance to do. After about four weeks my boss said I'm off for three weeks, blimey, you had better show me which way to go then I said. Easy he said getting up from his desk and pointing to his seat sit there and face that way, and he was gone, talk about being in the deep end. I got my own desk after about three months and was told I had passed my probationary period. Thus started four years of a different life, no more out of town, home every night apart from when I had to stay away on business trips. Fancy me the kid from Aston talking business to Australian businessmen. Because I was now office based I had to kit myself out in office type clothes, this consisted of a short sleeved shirt and shorts with walk socks in the summer. It used to fascinate me that you would meet a client and he would have shorts on. Winter was just wearing what I thought of as usual clothes. Although one year someone started the fad of wearing a black leather jacket, you weren't anybody if you hadn't got a real leather coat. We had a contract in a place called Mount Gambier, this was about three hundred miles from Adelaide and by road you had to go down the Princes and Southern Ports Highways, which ran along the Coorong, this was a natural reserve running for miles along the Southern Ocean. All sorts of wildlife lived in this area and I saw kangaroos, pelicans, parrots, lizards and a multitude of other things. Generally though it was down there by plane every two weeks or so, at first I was delighted to be flying there but as it involved a seven o'clock flight in the morning and no return for twelve hours the delight soon wore off. We had won a contract in a place called Broken Hill which was in New South Wales, this was a silver mining town, mining anything is a tough job done by tough men, and these miners were no exception to the rule. It was as rough as any mining town anywhere and for some reason was governed by South Australia, this town was over three hundred miles from the office and because of the roads the preferred way of getting there was by air. On one of my trips I had spent the usual twelve hours in Broken Hill, it had been a long hot tiring day and I like I suppose the rest of the passengers on the plane was looking forward to getting home and to having a shower. The plane started its engines and we buckled up in anticipation, at that moment one of the male cabin staff came along the plane and stopped by the bloke who was in the seat immediately in front of me, he leant over and I heard him say to this man, we are not going to take you in the state you are in, it was only when he opened his mouth to reply I realised this bloke was drunk. F… off he said I paid my fare and I am not getting off, the crewmember sighed and vanished to be replaced by the Captain, same performance same reply. Now one or two of the passengers were adding their thoughts to the situation and things were appearing to get ugly. We waited and after about five minutes a small police sergeant came along the cabin, he stood by the drunk and spoke in a friendly manner, come along sir you are holding the plane up and it is going nowhere with you on board. F… off I have paid and I am not moving, the sergeant bent right over and whispered to this obstinate drunk, get off the f…ing plane or I will set Ben on to you, I wondered if Ben was a savage dog perhaps, no such worries on the drunks behalf, I am not moving, wearily the sergeant stood up and waved his hand towards the back of the plane. I sat there in suppressed excitement the dog will soon sort this bloke out. The lights in the cabin darkened and I looked back along the plane to see advancing towards us a man mountain he was that big he had to duck his head to get down the aisle and walk sideways to get through. He placed a dinner plate sized hand on the seat in front, and spoke quietly to the drunk, get off the plane you little shit or I will really sort you out, the drunk looked up and his survival instinct must have kicked and he seemed to immediately sober up by the sight of this human colossus, I'm going I'm going he said in a quavering voice, the giant led the way followed by the cowering drunk and the cocky little sergeant and not a few catcalls from the fed up passengers. I found out later that this copper and his sergeant only had to appear anywhere there was a punch up or trouble and it was soon resolved.

On another trip to Broken Hill the contract engineer who I was going to be travelling with said I have chartered a six seater plane to take us there and back, I have got two other blokes to go with us and it works out cheaper than a regular flight, also we can go when we like and come back as soon as we are done, this was a much better idea than hanging around for twelve hours. We met at a small airport and took off, I thought it was a great way to travel, nice and easy, go where you like and at a slow leisurely speed. There had been floods in the southeast that year and the engineer asked the pilot to fly over the area, Aussies don't see much flooding so it must have been a real sight to them. We got to the local airport and the pilot borrowed a car and dropped us off at the site. Where is the A/C unit asked one of the engineers who had flown with us, on the roof I said, he seemed to pale a little under his sun tan, are there stairs to the roof, no you will have to go up a ladder. I got a ten foot ladder and placed it against the building and went up it to the roof, come on then I said, he took one step onto the ladder and with a low moan literally froze, his arms clamped around the ladder and it looked as if I would need a crowbar to shift them. I had heard of this sort of thing before but had never encountered it. It took me about an hour to get this bloke up a ten-foot high ladder and into the tin housing where the unit was on the roof, but we did it in the end. A few hours later it was lunch and we went to the local pub for some food, we had ordered our lunch when I noticed the fear of heights man was missing, where's your mate I asked his colleague, bloody hell he must still be on the roof, I ran back to the site and climbed the ladder, the poor bloke was sat there as red as beetroot and sweating like a pig, I thought you would never come he groaned, it took ages to get him down from the roof and when his feet hit the ground he was off like a scalded rabbit to the pub, I have never seen a bloke scull a pint so quick as this bloke did, why have you got a job like that where you have to get onto roofs, I asked him, the money was the reply.

It was about this time in nineteen seventy three that the Labour Party got into power, they had gone into the election with the catchy phrase "Its Time" meaning it was time for a change. Although I had delivered blurbs on their behalf with the Pommy hater I didn't think they had a chance of getting in. Across the road from where we lived there was an office guy who was an out and out Liberal, and to wind him up the Pommy hater sent over a real dyed in the wool Labour bloke to ask him to join the Labour Party, the ensuing argument had most of the neighbours out listening, but we had to step in when it looked like blows would start. One of the draughtsmen told me to put my money where my mouth was about the election, I didn't think Labour would win and we had a five-dollar bet. I lost of course. I decided that to pay him the five bucks was too tame and as I had a welding kit at home I got five dollars worth of one and two cent coins and brazed them into the logo "Its Time Yes Its Time" and when he demanded his winnings I handed it over in front of all his mates. He seemed to be really put out but he had the last laugh as the tea lady who's old man was a Labour bloke bought it from him for ten dollars.

We had got to know a couple of Brummy families who lived locally, one was the father in law of Sheila's brother John. They had come to Aussie in 1972 and lived about half a mile away. Obviously John's wife had put some pressure on him to emigrate to Aussie so that she could be near her family, and in 1974 at Xmas they came over. They were followed into Darwin where they first landed by a Hurricane, which devastated parts of the city. They missed the storm by hours but it was a memorable landing. I picked them up from Adelaide airport, I don't like this place too much he said, give it a chance we replied. We gave them a real seafood meal that night and hoped they would soon settle in. Between us and the family next door we had purchased a little four seater dingy complete with oars, we would go down on the local Onkaparinga River and fish there for hours, we never caught much but it was fun. My next door mate said I have bought a fishing net do you fancy going night fishing, of course, invite that brother in law of yours he said we need at least three blokes to do it properly. That weekend we took off down south to a place called Willunga beach, this was a flat expanse of beach where you could walk out quite easily for a good distance it was ideal for launching the little dingy, my Aussie mate explained what we had to do, the net was carefully placed on the back of the boat with one end secured to it, then we would push out through the surf the guy who was going to row the dinghy, the Aussie went first, he vanished into the darkness and surf and then rowed parallel to the beach whilst we hung onto the net. When the net had all gone he turned to shore and rowed in, everyone then got the ends of the net and pulled like mad. A single fish was the result of all our efforts, never mind said my mate its your turn, we reloaded the net and I set out, I had to row like mad to get past the surf but once past it the sea was fairly calm. I rowed down the beach till the net had gone then came in. I had got even less than my mate, nothing at all, ever the optimist my mate turned to the brother in law, your go. Same performance a push through the surf and he vanished into the darkness of the night, we left the kids hanging onto the net and strolled down the beach to where we thought he may land, we stood there in the pitch darkness listening to the surf, he's been gone a long time said the unworried Aussie, we went back to where the kids were and tested the net, it felt firm so it wasn't adrift, we gave a real heave on the line and this produced a faint cry from out of the blackness of the sea nowhere near where we thought he should be. You will have to go and get the stupid bastard, so out I went I hung onto the net and walked straight out, the noise of the surf was now behind me and I could hear him shouting help. I finally got to him apparently instead of rowing parallel with the beach he had lost his bearings and gone straight out. And somehow he had got the net caught around his neck so that every time the tide surged or we pulled the net it would nearly strangle him. We got back to the shore and pulled in the net and there under the torchlight gleamed a large eyeball staring up at us, what the hells that I said jumping back, it's a squid said my mate and I love them, you can have the thing. We finally caught a couple of dozen fish, which made the trip worthwhile, and we had many a trip after that. In the good ship Tigger.

In nineteen seventy two the Queen came over to Australia and followed the route that Captain Cook had taken, this involved a visit to Glenelg a place where we had stayed when we first arrived. The Aussies generally took the mickey out of the Royal family but the thousands who turned up to see her that day couldn't all have been Brits. One of our projects which the Queen was due to officially open was a place called the Festival Theatre a wonderful building right by the Adelaide Oval cricket ground. We had installed water fountains as a feature around the theatre and the Queen would press a button and up the water would go. Unfortunately we had not been able to get the proper pumps to the site and so had rigged up a temporary system, we had tested it and it worked. I was on a two-way radio to the man who had installed the job, and when the Queen pushed the button I told him to turn on the pumps, all went well. Between the Festival Theatre and the Houses of Parliament adjacent to it we were picking up some real big contracts, It still gives me a real thrill to see these two buildings on the telly whenever we play cricket or the city of Adelaide is shown, and all run by my boss and me. We had started a huge prestige project and I was asked to run it as an on site supervisor, it was a largest bus depot in the State and one of the biggest contracts our company had ever won. I was pleased to be asked but felt I was being used a little especially as I had now got my own desk in the communal office and felt I was a real office wallah. On site we were a real mixed bunch, English, Australian, German, Italian, Russian, Irish, Greek, Scots, Croatian, and Yugoslav, the food at mealtimes was strange and varied, try this said one, you try this one then, the United Nations had nothing on us and we were a little happy band of warriors. The job progressed nicely, there was a lot of gas welding under the floor in the service pits where the buses ran over to be serviced, the hydraulic pipe work had to be tested to ten thousand P.S.I. There wasn't a pump in Aussie that was able to produce these pressures and we had to get one from America. One day one of the English lads, who was returning to the UK that weekend said I have hurt my back, can you give me a job sitting down. I must say I took a dim view of his request but as he was off that week I sent him under the floor to sit and weld pipes. Later on he gave me a shout, can you help me with a length of pipe, we got it from the stores and he led the way back to his working area rubbing his bad back as he did so, he had to bend over to get to his work area, and as he did so he dropped the pipe onto his foot, he immediately tried to stand up and smashed his head on the low concrete ceiling, from where I stood it looked like a comedy scene from some mad film Charlie Chaplin silent film, and when he staggered out from under the floor, he was trying to hold his head rub his back and hop on one foot, and all the time giving out low moans, I was in bits, I couldn't stand for laughing and he didn't improve matters when he started swearing at me. I took him to hospital where they confirmed he had broken his big toe; they stitched up his head wound and gave him some ointment for his back. I found it immensely funny and still laugh at the scene yet. One day we were testing an outside underground fire main which ran around the bus station and was about a kilometre long, I had filled it with water and was applying pressure via the American pump. My right hand man this day was a tall lanky laconic Australian, have a walk around and see if you can see any obvious leaks I told him, he meandered off into the distance taking his job seriously and peering down the trench as he went. I watched him as I had a fag and stood by the pump, he was at the furthest point from me when I saw him suddenly look down into the trench, and then he dropped to his knees to inspect the problem further, suddenly and magnificently as if in a first World war silent film he was engulfed with a huge volcanic spout of water and mud, he vanished under this unexpected deluge, only to emerge walking away from the scene, my ribs hurt that much from laughing that I collapsed, he finally approached me wringing wet and with mud dripping from his eyebrows, I think I've found a leak. A typical Aussie understatement I thought. I had asked the boss if we could work a few Saturdays and he agreed. I arranged with our office to get the builder to open up the gate and we all rolled up on the first Saturday to find the site completely locked, obviously no one had told the builders, no problem I thought we will have to go under the gate which was high off the ground. I went under first and as I stood up a broad Black Country voice said freeze, I looked round to where the sound had come from and advancing towards me was a small security guard clutching a gun in his outstretched hands peering at me through large black specs. Are you kidding I asked him, don't move was the reply, either shoot me or put that thing away I said, we are supposed to be working here this morning, and it looks like no one told your mob, get on the blower and sort it out, there was no way I felt threatened by this little Black Country bloke and his big gun, it was too funny. He ordered me back under the fence and went to phone up his company. After about ten minutes he reluctantly opened the gate for us. We went to take down the eight by four sheets of plywood from the entrance to the building and as we did so a gust of wind blew one of the supporting planks over, this unfortunately landed edgeways on the three little toes on my right foot, I made no reaction and we all stood looking down at the plank, finally someone said didn't that hurt? I leant down and took the offending plank off my foot, and waved my hands to them to clear a gap and when they had done so I gave a huge scream and did a one legged Chinese dance around the area. I heard a snigger and looked around, the little gunslinger was laughing as he looked out of his office window. I think this hurt me more than my foot, fancy letting a Black Country bloke have the last laugh over you. I went to the hospital where an X-ray showed I had flattened and broken my three little toes, there's nothing we can do with this lot said the Doctor just have three weeks off and go back when they stop hurting, I hopped painfully away, that will teach me to laugh at other peoples misfortunes I thought. I took his advise but after about a week of Sheila hitting my broken toes with the vacuum cleaner and anything else she could get her hands on I went back.

A NEAR THING OR TWO.

I had driven down to our job in Mount Gambier and stayed the night with the lads, I was allowed to take some expenses for entertainment so I would take about fifty dollars, put it on the bar and invite all the lads to have a drink, much Amber Nectar was imbibed on these occasions. Later the following afternoon, I was driving my car back from Mount Gambier and was doing about ninety on the clear straight road. I had stopped for lunch at the only café within miles and was half way home on the picturesque Coorong when I noticed rain clouds about five miles up ahead where the road rose over the rolling hills. I made a mental note to slow down as I got near to the hills, when I reached the slopes of the hills I slowed to about seventy and as I did the rain began to really pelt down, I hit a slow left hand bend and noticed that the tarmac changed colour from black to red just ahead, I immediately knew I was in serious trouble. As I hit the red tarmac I lost control of the car, it shot right across the road and went onto the dirt shoulder, everything was in slow motion by this time and I remember trying to avoid a large wooden stump that was sticking up. I jerked the wheel to the right, but this reaction sent the car up the forty five degree rock face and the car rolled, it came down with a smash up side down and I managed to shut my eyes and duck my head as the roof caved in and the windscreen broke into a thousand bits which flew into the car. The car spun two or three times and came to a halt, I sat there a little bit disorientated strapped in as I was and upside down, my most uppermost thought was to get out of the vehicle in case it set on fire, I unbuckled the belt and dropped to the ceiling of the car, I intended to go out through the windscreen area but this was squashed down, I looked towards the door and as I did so a pair of legs appeared from the knees down, a voice shouted are you alright in there, yes thank you do you think you could open the door so I can get out. He pulled the door open and I climbed out, and then reached back in for my glasses and fags and matches, Jesus mate we thought you were dead, there were two blokes and they just stood there mouths agape. I moved away from the car and lit a cigarette, when I looked around I saw just how lucky I had been, the car was upside down on the dirt track by the side of the road, it was on a blind bend for anyone coming the other way and if any vehicle had been there at the same time it would surely have hit me head on. I shook hands with these two guys, thank you so much. My rescuers made sure I was OK and then because they were in a hurry made off, I stood by the side of the road in the pouring rain feeling cold wet and miserable, but also strangely elated that I was still here to be wet. A car came over the hill and pulled over, it was the owners of the café I had been in that day, are you all right, yes thank, do you want us to get a tow truck organised from the nearest Town which was a place called Meningie. Yes please. I had to wait about three hours for the police and tow truck to arrive, whilst I was waiting every vehicle that passed me stopped, even the big trucks I could hear them changing down through the gears and then a few minutes later the truck would arrive, you all right mate, yes thank you. I couldn't imagine anything like this happening in the UK but on the Aussie country roads it was the norm. The police had to block off the highway as the tow truck righted the car and lifted it onto the bed of the truck. So here I was stuck in Meningie miles away from home, I hadn't got a lot of cash on me and anyway there were no buses or trains. The bloke who had towed in the car said do you want us to take your vehicle to Adelaide for you, we discussed the cost and it was favourable, we have got a truck going down there tonight so we will put it on that. Is there any chance of me going with the truck I asked, sure mate no worries. I got to Adelaide at about eleven o'clock that night, and got a taxi home from where he had dropped me. I think the after shock must have set in then because I drank loads of the Amber Nectar to settle my jangling nerves and kept Sheila up half the night going over and over the tale. I had a complete set of X-rays done the next day and a full check up, the only thing that could be seen was a small cut on my cheek and bruises across my chest from where the seat belts had done their job. It seemed the only thing that was really hurt was my pride. Because she worked in Adelaide I asked the brother in laws wife Moe to give my car a tow back home, she agreed and we met where the car had been stored, and because it had no windscreen it was very windy and cold. She got us through the city no problems at all, I thought what a credit to her driving so carefully, carefully that is till she hit the South Road a wide dual carriageway. It was at this point that she seemed to have forgotten that I was a captive audience and just as it started to rain buckets she put down her foot. Now not only was I freezing but I was getting drowned as well, I had to take my glasses of and having a fag was out of the question. This nightmare trip continued till she pulled up at a set of lights and I slowly banged into her rear bumper, I saw her hands go up in the air as she realised I was still attached to her car, we finished the trip at a more sedate rate and when she got me to my place I got out of the car like a drowned rat and let the rain out of the car by opening the door with my frozen talon like hands, I think the trip home was more frightening than the actual accident, but I didn't tell her of course.

Our garden when we moved in was on a split level, the back being about fifty feet wide, I decided to grow vegetables on part of it and so we started to clear out the weeds and rubbish left by the previous tenants. Up one end of the garden was a lot of limestone rocks and when I turned over one of them there was a nest of red back spiders, my shovel and fear soon put an end to them though. It turned out that there was a layer of black soil about nine inches deep and under that it was limestone. We moved a load of soil onto one spot for a veggie patch and then grassed the rest. We had never had a real garden before and we spent about two weeks pulling up weeds by hand, the Pommy hater watched with interest, when we had finally got rid of the weeds he said why didn't you hire a rotary hoe? A rotary hoe? What's one of those? I got my little fenced off patch going and successfully grew, tomatoes, lettuces, beetroot, peas, dwarf beans, carrots, radishes and lots of bits and pieces, we felt so good actually growing our own stuff. Because of the wonderful climate we felt we could grow anything, and certainly successfully tried a lot of different things. Sheila has got real green fingers and I used to think if she planted a match it would grow. We had a rabbit called Bugs, who was free to roam the garden, he dug a burrow that deep I couldn't reach the bottom even with a broom handle, we had a cat called Tigger and a couple of ducks, and a four foot long aquarium, Sheila had got a job at the local slaughterhouse along with her brother, she started on the floor where the meat from the killings came to but then had a transfer to the small goods department, and he was helping clear up after the slaughter men had done their bit, the hardest part he said was trying to pick up the rubbery udders, it took him some time to realise they were taking the piss out of him and trying to wind him up. Sheila would bring home all sorts of meats, hams, veal, pork, bacon I was spoilt for choice for my lunches. Things were really looking up for us now, we had two cars, both of us were working, the kids were established at local schools. Most weekends we would take off in the car to explore where we lived, I would say to one of the kids which way off the drive, left, so left it would be, at the end of the street, which way, right, so right it would be and we would proceed like this for hours, it led to some very strange places but it was different. When we had moved into this house there had been no drive just a dirt strip, and once when it rained over night I had got bogged in and had to get towed out by my mate over the road. We finally saved the money to have a nice concrete drive put in and we really felt posh. About this time skateboards were making an appearance and because we lived on a hill the kids would use our drive as a starting point to go down the hill, they would go about four houses down and turn up a neighbours drive. I watched them playing when one of them challenged me to have a go, easy peasy I said although I had never been on one before. I stood gingerly on the skateboard and pushed off, I turned left off the driveway and as I looked down the three hundred yard long hill it suddenly seemed as steep as the slopes of Everest, fear gripped me but I couldn't show it, Ill just go to the drive and turn up there I thought, I may have thought it but the G force my weight had created said different, I whizzed past the safe haven of the neighbours drive to the excited shouts of the kids following in my wake, go for it Mr Twist, great ride dad, my toes tried to grip the board through my shoes as I really picked up speed, I flew down the hill at what seemed like a hundred miles an hour, people watched as this mad skateboarder arms akimbo sped past, a couple of dogs appeared from nowhere and tried to catch me, no chance, the uneven flagstones rattled my clenched teeth, the houses flashed past in a blur, I got to the bottom of the hill and my well honed self preservation instincts kicked in, I managed to lean to the left and vanish up the hill from the following chasing kids view. I came to a gentle halt the sweat running into my eyes, and knees trembling picked up the board and casually walked back around the corner, to the resounding cheers of the kids and the applause of the amazed neighbours, and for quite some time I was their hero. Over the hill the other way I had made friends with a bloke who used the local pub, and was a member of the local boys football team as was I, he was a big bloke, blonde haired and blue eyed, he was an ex boxer and as hard as nails, like most hard men he was as soft as putty when it came to his kids, but he was also a great laugh, he was always cracking jokes, and was well known for playing practical jokes on people and was full of funny stories. One Saturday afternoon the Pommy hater stuck his head over the fence, want a quick game of pool? I'm going for some beer and I fancy a game, too right. We got down the pub and my long haired mate was also there, so were a couple of Taffy's from the local rugby club, they were a good bunch of blokes and I had watched them play a couple of times. One of them a solid sort of bloke was very much the worse for wear, his mates tried to get him out of the pub when they went but he was having none of it. I got him a chair to sit on and asked him if he had his car there, yes. I knew he lived in the street where I had gone up on the skate board, he couldn't drive in that state and I said look we are going in about half an hour just hang on and we will give you a lift. We played our games and after half an hour or so we were ready to go, I looked all round for the rugby player but he was nowhere to be seen. As we walked through the drive in part of the pub one of the bar staff who lived in our road said you own the Valiant don't you to the Pommy hater, yes, well it looks like someone has hit it on the way out of the car park. My long haired mate who was with us couldn't help but laugh, he knew the Pommy hater loved his big American car, the barman continued, he then reversed into a white Holden, the smile vanished from my other mates face. We went out to the car park and fair enough both cars had been hit, what the odds were of hitting two cars that were not even close to each other, and owned by neighbours was anybody's guess, but he had done it, the damage was not too bad as it turned out, and there was blue paint on both the cars. Two guys were stood there did you see who did this by any chance? Yes it was a thickset bloke wearing a black T-shirt. The description fitted the rugby player. I know him I said lets call in on him and we wont have to get the cops involved, they both agreed. We drove round to the rugby player's house and there he was still sitting in his car, a ding with red paint in it on the front of his car, and a ding with white paint in it on the back. The Pommy hater wasted no time, I want you to accept responsibility for hitting my car, the drunk looked up, F*** off he said I hit nothing, my long haired mate who also knew him said you hit my car as well, this was obviously too much information for the inebriated man, and you can F*** off too he said. I knocked the rugby players door and his wife came out, look I said you can clearly see where he has hit both cars, all you have to do is tell these two that it will be sorted out tomorrow provided he accepts he did it. She saw the logic in the argument but pissed up hubby obviously didn't, I did not hit your cars he said staggering past the glaring evidence, and he then made a move that was to cost him a fortune in the future, he grabbed the Pommy hater and my long haired mate by the front of their shirts pulled them both towards him then pushed them back. The results were that both of them lost their shirts. The Pommy hater didn't hesitate, that's it I'm off to the cops are you coming he asked me, yes Ill go with you. We went to the local police station where my neighbour reported the whole incident to the sergeant behind the desk, leave it to us sir. The drink drive laws were very strict at that time and the cops were at his house in no time and he was arrested on the spot. The rugby player got six weeks in the nick, a thousand dollar fine for being drunk in charge of a vehicle and not reporting an accident, and banned for a year. After that the other rugby players wouldn't talk to me they thought I had dobbed him in because all he could remember about the incident was that it was my long haired neighbours mate, which as far as they were concerned was me. When he came out of the nick he came up to talk to the Pommy hater about the incident, you cost me a fortune he said I was self employed and now I have to get a job working for someone else and they have to pick me up every day the Pommy hater eyed him up coldly and said, if your wife had have listened to Graham and you had accepted that you would pay for the damage none of this would have happened, but you didn't listen and it did happen and it was all your own fault so you can piss off and don't try to blame us for you being drunk. And another thing if you come here again I will call the cops on you. The rugby player must have finally seen sense because he just turned on his heel and went.

ANOTHER JOB.

I had been in my job four years now and felt I was part of the furniture, I had my own desk and was estimating, purchasing, and controlling my own contracts. So it was with some surprise to me that I was again asked to run a large contract as an on site Supervisor, I was not taken with the idea at all and let my thoughts be known to my boss and the branch manager, as far as I was concerned my job was office based. We had a meeting and I said I felt I was being got at, especially as we had men quite capable of running a site like this. The branch manager said it was a real prestige contract and we cannot afford to cock it up, take have a week off while we all think about it, go and throw pebbles on a beach somewhere. I took a week off and when I returned we had another meeting have you changed your mind I was asked, no was the reply, well we want you to run this site said the manager, I dug in, sorry I said there is no way I am going to do it. Thus my career as an office wallah came to an abrupt end. So now here I was out of work once again, but it was a situation I was not unused to and in a week I got a job on the tools with a large company. There was a Kiwi in charge of this contract and when he found out I had run bigger jobs than this one he asked me to sort out the plant room. The plant room on any site is the heart of the job and the most complicated so I was more than pleased to oblige. I had noticed a young bloke one day sweeping up the work area, why is he doing that I asked if he's an apprentice, nobody wants to work with him they think he's mad. Just my sort of bloke I thought, he was about six feet tall, good-looking and with a beard, his main problem it seemed was because he was a biker. No sweat to me, it was a strange fact about apprentices in Aussie that if the work got short or their face didn't fit then the Employer could send them to another company, all they were obliged to tell the apprentice was where he had to go. The lad had been under this threat and having sympathy with the under dog, I insisted he became my mate, and like anyone who felt ostracised he responded positively and turned out to be one of the hardest grafters on the company. One day I was on the top of a large copper tank and feeling in a bit of a daft mood I was dancing a soft shoe shuffle, all the blokes on one side were having a laugh at this, what I hadn't noticed was that the Managing Director and some of his cronies including my Supervisor had entered the room behind me, what are you doing asked the Supervisor, caught bang to rights I said this is called the soft shoe shuffle don't you know it. There were peals of laughter from the workers side and I noticed even the MD had to turn away with a grin. The Supervisor just waved his hand at me to get off the tank. My mate came in one Monday looking a bit off, what's the matter, I got nicked the weekend for showing a brown eye to a copper, I looked into his hazel eyes, a brown eye so what, you don't understand he said a brown eye is when you drop your trousers and show your bare arse, apparently some of his biker mates had dared him to moon at passing cars by shoving his bum out of the car window, unfortunately for him one of them was an unmarked cop car and showing your bum to passing police cars was a real no no. We finally finished this contract and I was asked to go and work with my biker mate up the bush at a place called Wudinna. This place was a small town on the Eyre Peninsula and the contract was a local school. We stayed at the only hotel in town and soon started playing pool for them, the away games were interesting and you could travel anything up to fifty miles for a match. Huge amounts of the Amber Nectar was consumed on these journeys and it was a wonder we never killed others or ourselves on the way back, but you don't get many cars on the road at midnight up the bush. I was up the bar one night when three blokes walked in, they had arrived that day and had were staying at the hotel I got to talking to them, what do you do then? We walk the line was the enigmatic reply, walk the line? What do you mean? It turned out that they worked for the Government Telephone Company and it was their job to itemise everything that was by the side of the road between the telegraph poles. They had a chain that was one furlong long, one would stand on the end whilst the other paid out the chain from the back of the vehicle, then the third man who was a draftsman who would drive slowly along the length of the chain and draw on a map anything of interest ie: a gate or a dirt track, bushes or trees. They had started in Western Australia and were going up to New South Wales; they had been at it for months and still had months to go. What a job. Although Wudinna was only a small place there always seemed to be something happening, for instance every six weeks or so little planes flew in and pickup trucks arrived, for the local Corroboree, just an Aboriginal name for a big booze up. These events were great and gave me real insight into the Aussie character. It was during one of these nights that I was in the bar talking to two of the Interstate walkers when the local bully an immensely powerful looking foul mouthed person shouted across the bar at us, I want a piece of you you bastard he said looking towards us his drunken eyes not really focusing on any one of us, I quivered slightly, I don't mean you hook nose he shouted to one of the blokes who had a big conk, and I don't mean you four eyes which was me, I mean Buffalo Bill there pointing to our third partner, I must say he did look a bit like the cowboy, he had long hair and a small beard and moustache, and was wearing an Aussie slouch hat. I moved slightly to the right away from the intended victim, the cowboy who was at least a foot shorter than the bully coolly looked at him, anytime you like, I moved further to one side, the bully shouted Ill sort you out later and went back to his beer. The night wore on, later on the local plumber who I had got to know came over, he was a big man too, don't worry about him he said if he starts on you lot Ill sort him out, I am the only one who can handle him, I breathed a sigh of relief, I wasn't too worried I lied, but I think he saw the naked fear in my eyes, OK he said and walked away. My two drinking partners had been talking amongst themselves, we have got a plan said hook nose, in the back of the car we have got a pickaxe handle what we want you to do is to lure him outside, we will do the rest, we are off in the morning and he will never find us. Although I had consumed large amounts of the Amber Nectar this plan seemed to have a flaw in it somewhere, you want me to get him outside and you will sort him out? Yes. I pondered over this simple idea, it seemed as if it might work then it suddenly it struck me, you pair are leaving in the morning, right, right, but that leaves me here on my own to face the bully when he figures out who lured him outside, what's the matter said the cowboy, you gutless? Suddenly sober I nodded and the plan died the death. Nothing untoward happened that night and the walkers left the next day. When we had first booked into the hotel there had been a meeting of salesmen there, these blokes would be on the roads for weeks and would end up at this hotel about once every two months. There were about eight of them, they didn't talk shop they just wanted to let their hair down and get pissed amongst their own kind. I was playing pool when one challenged me to a game, I beat him, play you for a drink he said, your on, I beat him, play you for five dollars he said, your on, I beat him, bloody hell he said I'm having no luck at all tonight, why what else have you lost at, see that Sheila over there he said pointing to a good looking young lady who had salesmen hanging around her like bees round a honey pot, I hadn't seen on the other side of the room, for six months now we have been running a book as to who will get her into bed first, tonight it was my turn to try and she knocked me back flat. I took another look over and vaguely noticed my mate hovering around the sellers fringe. I went to bed, and when I got up in the morning I went to wake my mate as usual to find he wasn't there and his bed hadn't been slept in. Puzzled I went down for breakfast and there sitting at the table with the happy looking young lady was my mate, he looked at me and winked, then smirked at the glowering sales men and if looks could kill he would have died an instant thousand painful deaths from the jealous salesmen's eyes. One night they held an Hunts mans Ball at the local hall and although we had no tickets we managed to get in some how. Everyone bar us was dressed in hunting gear with the ladies in long dresses and really looked the part. Funny enough even though we stuck out like a dogs nuts I felt no embarrassment at all amongst these easy going Australian country folk.

A LOSS OF TWO MATES, AND A GAME OF POOL.

Life was carrying on quite nicely and in April it was Sheila's birthday, we had decided to go for a meal at the local pub and just as we were leaving the house it came over the radio that someone had been shot and killed in an accident in O,Sullivans Beach. As we drove over the hill to get to the pub there were a couple of police cars parked outside the barman's house. We both thought that he was the person who had had the accident so we were more than surprised when we saw him serving behind the bar. I thought you were dead I said, no he said it was the bloke across the road, so the police hadn't parked on the side where the accident had occurred. It turned out it was the practical joking boxer, surrounded by his wife and kids he had been playing with an old rifle which he had owned for years, it was supposedly unusable couldn't fire and had a cartridge jammed up the spout. He had been pretending to be a soldier and was sloping arms and all the rest of it when he slammed the gun down on the floor. This fired the jammed bullet and it went up through his throat killing him instantly. The only consolation was he was with the people he loved when it happened. It seemed a terrible waste of such a nice hard working dad, he had a massive turn out to his funeral and his death was reported in all the local papers, which was a fitting tribute to him.

I was pretty good at pool and when I was at home I played for the local pub team, one day one of the lads said we have started up two teams and we want you to run the B-side. I readily agreed, my team turned up later that week for practice, and what a mixed bunch, one was an American high school teacher, one a dustman, my long haired mate from across the road, a mechanic and various other individuals. I tried to gather them together for a pep talk, waste of time, half were already under the influence of the Amber Nectar and the rest were rapidly trying to catch them up. It seemed that the only common denominator we all had was an unnatural love of the Amber Nectar, and being competitive types they were always trying to outdo each other in the boozing department. We would play other local teams and because we all knew each other there was no mercy asked and none given. Match rules were strictly adhered to and everyone was a barrack room lawyer and knew them by heart and were not afraid to voice them to the referees. Because of our fondness for the drink I found I had to pick my team with their ability to take the drink in mind. Thus those who could stay sober longest played last. Against all the odds we actually reached the final of a cup game, this was to be played at a rival neutral pub. I told my crew not to get there too early; I didn't want the dreaded drink to interfere with our playing ability. Some hopes, the opposing team went all out to knobble my players, plying them with free drinks and much false camaraderie, the game proceeded with my plan of playing the soberest persons last looking as if it may work. The bloke who was the referee that night was a well-known, well-liked drunk. He stood by the head of the table arms crossed leaning on the rest occasionally making decisions. During my game I needed the rest and putting my hand out towards the ref said rest please, I had no response so I walked up to him took the rest from under his arms and turned around to take my shot. Suddenly there was a huge crash behind me and I turned round to see the ref flat out on the floor amid a rising cloud of dust, arms still folded, obviously he had taken the word rest literally because that what he had been doing. We slowly got him up to his wobbly feet and legs but he seemed a bit upset about the sniggers and outright laughter that echoed around the pub. After that the refs decisions seemed to go against us, but in the fullness of time and remembering through a fog of alcohol I will give him the benefit of the doubt. We were drawing three each and it was the Yanks turn to play the deciding game with one of our better players, the Yank swaggered up to the table swishing and flourishing his cue as if it was an extension of his arm, for all the world looking like a gunman from the OK corral. G-day folks he said in his broad Texan accent, turned round to address the balls most professionally before promptly falling onto the table dead drunk, there was an uproar of laughter from the opposition, and groans of despair from our mob, the game was abandoned and I watched the large silver cup being handed over to the opposing captain, the knobblers had done a great job. A taste of ashes but I was proud of my team none the less. We had saved a few dollars with every game we had played and by popular vote we were to have a bar-b-que at one of the lads houses, there was a fifty seven gallon barrel of beer with cooling equipment. It was to be on a Saturday night and we were all looking forward to it. We had a great time and by eleven o'clock I had had enough and went home, my long haired mates wife came over the next day, do you know where he is she asked he hasn't been home all night, blimey isn't he back yet, I went round to the scene of the party and there sat around the barrel was four blokes, your missus wants you home I said, I aint going till the barrel is emptied his boozing partners nodded solemn drunken agreement, I left them to it, it took another day to drain the barrel, and I have to take my hat off to the resilience and perseverance and bloody mindedness of the Aussie piss pot. My longhaired mate had a party one night; I want you to meet a couple of mates of mine who are up from Western Australia. I met his two mates, one was of an ordinary size but the other one had what was called sheep Shearer,s hands, they were almost double the size of most peoples. During the night when the drink was flowing I was talking to the sheep Shearer's hand man, he said I'm going to give him a Meningie Pisser indicating my long haired mate, what's one of those I asked, watch he said. My mate like all of us was wearing shorts, the Shearer's hand man crept up behind him then crossing his huge hands he grabbed my mate by the soft flesh on the upper inside part of his legs and squeezed, the scream that came from my mate made everybody jump, five minutes later on the insides of his thighs two black, blue and red bruises appeared shaped perfectly like the Shearer's hand man. I had asked the big boy why he had left Western Australia and his reply was strange to say the least, apparently when they were working on the top of these silos the blokes would take loads of bottles of beer to the top and drink them during the day, a combination of booze in the hot sun and a new charge hand seemingly turned out too much for the lad and his mate, well what happened then I asked, were you sacked, no he said he fell off the silo and was killed. It was one of my birthdays and I invited my longhaired mate for a drink down the local and surprise surprise he declined the offer, he didn't show up at the party either. This was so unusual it was a real talking point that night. The next night and not long after the Meningie Pisser incident I was sat watching the telly at about ten o'clock at night when suddenly I heard screaming and the front door was hammered and the bell was rung frantically, I opened it and it was my long haired mates wife with their son, he's shot himself she shouted, I raced across the road and burst into the lounge area and there on the floor with blue grey and red matter pumping out of the back of his head lay my mate, his eyes were open but seeing nothing and he was labouring for breath. A revolver lay by his right hand, now was not the time to panic, I took out his false teeth to aid his breathing and then ran into the kitchen and got a tea towel,

I pressed it against the wound behind his right ear and tried to stop the bleeding. I picked up the phone and rang the emergency number and spoke to the operator, how can I help him I asked, you are doing all you can he said there is an ambulance on the way. The ambulance eventually arrived and they loaded my mate into it, I am going with him I said to Sheila could you get someone to pick me up at the hospital which was in Adelaide. They had put a rubber sheet over the stretcher and as the ambulance took off we tried to keep him alive, I was pumping his chest and the young ambulance man was getting air into his lungs, the rubber sheet slowly filled up with his blood and I realised that every time I pumped his chest I was actually pumping out his life's blood. I told the young ambulance man who was actually crying, carry on he said, we had gone about ten miles when I felt my mates soul leave his body, I gave up pumping immediately, what's happened said the ambulance man, he's gone I said. God rest his soul. It was strange where he passed away because we were only about half a mile from where his parents lived. This was one of the worst nights of my life in Aussie and it still gets to me even now, when you have no immediate family, friends become that much more important to you and my hairy mate was very important to me. We had had a lot of great times together and I knew I would really miss him. I had to go to see the Police Sergeant at the Station and give him an account of what had happened as far as I was concerned. When I had finished making my statement he said it was obviously suicide, I was very mindful of the Insurance Company's policies and their reluctance to pay out money when suicide could be proved, so I instantly objected, well what else could it be asked the Officer, did you have a good look at the chair he was sat in I asked, he shook his head, then I suggest you go and have look at it. My mate had got one of those chairs that reclined when you leant back on it, I suggested to the Officer that what had happened was that he had leant back too quick and because he was holding the gun in his right hand it was a natural reaction to throw up your hands, and this was where he had accidentally shot himself. The Coroners verdict was Accidental Death.

WORK AND A HOLIDAY UP THE BUSH

We were still working up the bush and the pub seemed to be like a light to a moth, the moths in this instant being some real characters. One of the carpenters on the job would walk around the site smelling like a marijuana plant, he reeked of the stuff, he was also wild eyed and always carried his axe whether at work or not on his belt day and night. I had tried to avoid him on site because of his reputation but then bumped into him in the pub one night, you a Pom, the inevitable question, yes but I've been here years I replied no doubt impressing him with my Brummy accent. He nodded and we carried on talking about the job and various other things, we had been rattling for about an hour and I was beginning to think all the bad things I had heard about him and his axe were pure nonsense. Just then a small youngish very pregnant girl walked into the bar, we all looked at her, here comes the littlest shag in Town I whispered hoping her husband if he was there wouldn't hear me. That's my wife said the wild eyed axe man gripping his deadly weapon, my back was against the wall and my rubber legs had a job holding me up, I know I said I was only pulling your leg. After what seemed an age the moment passed but I never spoke out of turn after that. One day at breakfast there was a longhaired bearded deeply suntanned bloke sitting at one of the tables, who's he I asked the bloke serving the breakfast, he's a real bush baby he said, he works the fence, works the fence? What's that? Why don't you ask him later on when he's in the bar? I decided to do just that and made a point of standing by him in the bar that night, G, day mate I said, he nodded and I started to bend his ear, we are here working on the school what do you do for a living, I repair the fence, what fence? He looked at me and said the Dingo fence he managed not to say stupid, oh where's that then, he took what I thought was a deep breath, it's a fence that runs from Western Australia to New South Wales its about three thousand miles long and it keeps the Dingoes out of the Southern states, my patch is about one hundred and fifty miles long and runs parallel to the Nullarbor Plain. Well what do you do then, he sighed, I check the fence for holes, then when the sand dunes blow against it I higher it, when they vanish I lower it. He lived in a tent for three months at a time and would only approach civilisation when he had to. He looked at me sadly, turned away and peered into his glass; I think I understood then why he preferred the solitude of the outback.

Back home we had a twenty four feet long by sixteen foot wide garage erected in the back garden, only it wasn't a garage it was a sports room, I had two ordinary sized doors put in it, and inside there was a dart board, a full sized table tennis set and a proper slate bed eight by four pool table, this was in the centre of place and was the most used piece of equipment in the room. It was my pride and joy and had cost a lot of money to buy and have installed.

We would play pool on a Friday night, there would be me, the brother in law, the Pommy hater, and a couple of guys I had worked with who lived locally, there were some epic pool sessions in this room. The Pommy hater not being too big a drinker usually won most of the loot and wasn't backwards in coming forward and telling me so the next hangover day. Sheila had got the gardens looking great and a lot of the weekends we spent going around gardening centres and the like. We didn't have money to burn but we could afford some of what we thought were the finer things in life. We both had cars and the kids were doing fine at their respective schools, we had built a wall around the split-level back garden and I had erected a large aviary. This aviary had Japanese partridge, zebra finches, canaries, and budgies. It was nice to wake up in the morning to a dawn chorus. Unfortunately it also attracted cats, and although I finally got rid of most of them there was one that lived over the back fence that would spend all night sitting on the roof of the aviary and prowling around frightening the birds. Drastic methods were required so I took advise off one of my Aussie mates, shoot the bloody thing he said, I don't want to kill it just frighten it away, he thought about it I will lend you an air gun, it wont kill the thing but it will give it a real shock. I took up his offer and sure enough when I shot the cat that was silhouetted in the moonlight it flew off the roof. I thought that was the end of the affair, but no, the next night it was back, same shot same result. I must have hit that flaming cat at least twenty times but it still came back for more. Finally I was able to get a device that gave cats a small electric shock when they got on the roof that stopped the thing. Christies Beach where we lived was quite a beauty spot and they would bring Aboriginal children down from the Northern Territory to have holidays there. It was a delight to see the little corn blonde haired kids faces as they looked on the sea for the very first time. We were all on the beach one day, swimming and messing about in Tigger when I heard a gang of six or seven guys who were getting stuck into the Amber Nectar talking, these Boongs are getting everywhere said one they sure are the others agreed (Boong was a name the white Aussies called the Aboriginals) I looked around me and couldn't see any Aboriginals, bloody Boongs said one looking directly at me, then I realised why they were saying it, I had long black hair at the time and the sea spray, salt and wind had blown it up into what looked like an Afro haircut, that combined with my going black in the Sun and I could see why they had mistaken me for an Aboriginal. Hot sun and the Amber Nectar were never good mates and I could see this could get ugly, then suddenly I had the answer I went and stood in front of them and dropping my trunks I showed them my bare white arse, I'm not a Boong I said, bloody hell mate sorry for that.

We had been offered a chance to rent a shack at a place called Point Soulter, this was on the Yorke Peninsular and overlooked the Spencer Gulf.

On the way to Point Sulter.

The shack was very basic but it was remote and very scenic. One day a small boat pulled into the bay, the bloke anchored up and then proceeded to gut his fish catch of the day. Later that day the kids noticed a big black shape glide into the area where the guts lay. It was a huge ray six feet across if it was an inch. After that we watched this ray come into the bay everyday at about the same time. We were walking along the beach one day when I found a flat stone and threw it towards the sea as I let go of it Grant appeared in my vision from the right, unfortunately the stone began to turn his way and I was running before it hit him. It caught him above the eye and bled quite badly, he still carries this scar to this day, and lesson learned never ever throw stones when there are kids about. One day when we were returning from a trip exploring the local area and we were about a mile from the shack there was a big bang from under the car, I got out and walking back found the silencer of the car lying in the dust.

Up the bush.

This in itself was not a major problem as I had some tools at the shack and knew I would be able to get it back on the car. What was a problem though was that as it came off the car it got trapped between the track and the petrol tank and had cut a hole like a half circle in the tank. The petrol was leaking out quite rapidly but having a spare can of juice on board I wasn't too bothered. I was bothered though as I went along because the gauge showed zero and the car ground to a halt. I knew the track ran uphill to the shack and as the hole was in the back I had the bright idea of driving backwards. I dropped of Sheila the two girls and Grant and taking Graham with me set of for Warooka which was the nearest little town, I had packed paper into the hole and just hoped it would hold. It did and we got into town on a Saturday afternoon. I drove to the garage, yes mate, I have punctured my petrol tank can it be fixed, lets have a look he said, he put the car on the hydraulic ramp and sent it into the air. He cast a professional eye over the cut, yep I can fix that, thank God for that I thought, I was thinking I would have to get a new tank. The mechanic got a piece of copper tube and flattened it, he then tinned it with solder, I was getting a little bit dubious by now as to how he was going to repair the hole. How are you going to fix it with that I asked, easy he said I'm going to solder it into position, soldering meant heat and even I knew heat and petrol did not mix, I had to get us away from this mad mechanic and I looked out of the garage doors in desperation, there across the square was a pub. We are thirsty I think we will just go and have a beer while you fix it. OK he said and grabbed his propane torch; we practically ran from the garage, I bought a beer and stood looking back at the garage from around a safe corner fully expecting an explosion at any time. Nothing happened and after a while my car was driven onto the forecourt. We sauntered casually back to the garage, you did it then I said, no problem was the reply I must get one of these a week, how much I asked, seven dollars I gave him ten. It was worth it for the lesson. While we were on this holiday a comet appeared in the sky and stayed in view for as long as we were there, it had a massively long tail and was quite a sight.

THE FINAL COUNTDOWN.

It was now late nineteen seventy-seven, the house was as complete as we could make it, the gardens were spot on and we had everything in the house and the games room that we felt we needed.

A last night with our Aussie neighbors

Both our cars were paid for and weekends were still spent watching the lads play football and going to garden centres. I had had another run in with authority and now found myself self employed, I had gone to sign on the dole but the paperwork to be filled in ran to pages and I did not feel inclined to do it, so I had a thousand pamphlets printed and me and the kids posted them out around the local area "You've tried the rest now try the best" not very original and as it turned out not very interesting. From all our hard work posting these things I got one reply and that was only about a leaking tap. I did pick up a job from a mate of mine about forty five miles away installing all the first fix plumbing in a house, it paid fifty dollars and to make it pay I would have to do it in a day, but any port in a storm I took it on. I worked really hard all that day without a break and by about five o'clock I had done all that had been asked of me. I was pooped, I got into the car and drove off, about a mile later there was a bloke thumbing a lift so I pulled over, G-day mate where you going, I was going right by where he wanted to go so told him to hop in. It was only when he sat in the car I realised that he and the Amber Nectar were not unknown to each other, in fact by the state of him they were inseparable partners. I tiredly drove on trying not to listen to his ramblings and probably because of this didn't notice the speed limit had changed as I went through a set of lights, and there on a street corner was a copper with a radar gun, up the road his mate walked into the road and put his hand out, the drunk said what's he want. I pulled over and wound the window down, do you realise you were speeding sir, and before I had a chance to reply the drunk shouted no we wasn't and a blast of Technicolor breath hit the officer full in the face, the cops face tightened, get out of the car and give me the keys, have you been drinking sir he asked me, no I haven't and I don't know who this bloke is either I am only giving him a lift. The upshot of the whole incident is I was fined fifty dollars so not only had I worked all day for nothing but I had points on my license as well. Not a great start for an enterprising Managing Director of a plumbing company. The Pommy hater who was a bricklayer by trade offered me some weekend work, I don't know if you will be up to it he said but its there if you want it, I gratefully accepted. We have got to lay the footings of a barn with brick piers, sounds easy to me I said, there are about two thousand bricks to be laid and I want to do them over the weekend. I had heard of brickies laying a thousand bricks in a day but had never seen it, I was about to get educated. We started at eight in the morning and I had to mix the cement and barrow the bricks to the demented Pommy hater who was laying bricks like a demented dervish octopus, by noon I was absolutely shattered, my legs were like rubber and my arms were falling off, I lay in the barrow feeling like a wet rag, cant take it eh? This turned out to be the spur I needed and I said there's no way you will get me packing it in. On the Sunday night he paid me the agreed money, you know he said I really never thought you would get through that lot, it's the hardest I have ever worked myself, so good on yer mate. My mouth said thanks but my broken back and four foot long arms said sod off.

I think the work doing the plumbing and then getting fined the same amount as I had earned left me disillusioned, and when you are in that frame of mind negative thoughts start to crowd into your mind. I found I began to worry a lot more about our families back home although we were in touch with them when we wanted to be by phone, little things that would never have bothered me in the past became real problems. I realise now that I had become severely homesick, nearly eight years had been a long time and although the living was much better than it would be in the UK it still wasn't home.

A view of Christies Downs from our house 1976

We held a family meeting and I'm afraid I ran roughshod over my children and my wife and all their objections, I had the bug and nothing was going to stop me having my way, I have regretted my bull headedness ever since but that was the way it was back then. We made arrangements to sell the house and in less than six weeks the very first person to look at it made us an offer which we accepted. We saw a travel agent and pencilled in a date to depart on the fifth of March nineteen seventy eight. That night I phoned the brother in law who's wife was pregnant and told him, book me on the same flight he said. I told him who the company was and left him to it. It seemed the whole street had heard we were going and a party was arranged in our honour. What a night everybody who we had made friends with over the years came to bid us farewell, including my best mate the Pommy hater from next door. They had made us a large cake and on it was an aeroplane, and the unforgettable words "Goodbye to the best Australians in the street" it was devastating.

Night out with some workmates 1975

The Pommy hater drove us to the airport no doubt pleased to see us go, and we hugged like two long lost brothers, the tears flowing freely. I said to him I will tell people the truth about you Aussies when I get back home. And here it is, once you got through their natural distrust of anything Pommy the Aussies we met were wonderful, warm, caring, considerate, hard, tough, independent, blunt, generous, funny, and kind, truly the salt of the Earth.

The plane landed at Heathrow exactly eight years to the day when we had landed in Adelaide, and as I kissed the ground my heart crept back into my body and I felt whole once again.